Praise for Brady Johns

"Brady Johns helped OneAffiniti expand into North America by building an outbound sales engine that way outperformed any of our expectations. His sales acumen and his ability to motivate sales teams are second-to-none."

—Joel Montgomery, Founder and CEO, OneAffiniti

"If you're like most of us, you've had it with fake experts parading around the internet, claiming to have the magic dust to make you rich. Brady Johns is the opposite—the only reason he isn't a household name is because he's busy actually doing the work! Brady is a great teacher, he's generous with his knowledge, and he has proven steps to generate massive success."

**—Jonathan Sprinkles, Founder, The Connection Lab
and two-time International Bestselling Author**

"I have received Brady Johns's counsel on real estate investments. He had the exact advice and direction I needed to succeed. Read, do, and follow through. And if you do so, I trust he can be a real boost to your learning as well."

—Luther Gabriel Biondo, Author of *Bridge of Fire*

"Brady Johns's financial wisdom was shared in a funny and approachable, yawn-proof way that kept me reading. I definitely attribute a significant portion of my own success IPOing two companies and the downstream financial wealth that resulted from it, to following his homespun Texas wisdom!"

**—Sherri Manning, Chief People Officer of
multiple technology companies**

FLIP-FLOPS AND FORTUNES

FLIP-FLOPS AND FORTUNES

Buy Your Life Back Through Real Estate
Investing and Passive Income Strategies

BRADY JOHNS

Matt Holt Books
An Imprint of BenBella Books, Inc.
Dallas, TX

Matt Holt is an imprint of BenBella Books, Inc.

10440 N. Central Expressway
Suite 800
Dallas, TX 75231
benbellabooks.com
Send feedback to feedback@benbellabooks.com

BenBella and *Matt Holt* are federally registered trademarks.

Printed in the United States of America
10 9 8 7 6 5 4 3 2 1

Library of Congress Control Number: 2022935022
ISBN 9781637741788 (hardcover)
ISBN 9781637741795 (ebook)

Copyediting by Sandra Wendel
Proofreading by Michael Fedison and Lisa Story
Text design and composition by PerfecType, Nashville, TN
Author photo by Justin Leitner, Score Headshots
Cover design by Brigid Pearson
Cover photography © Shutterstock / Proxima Studio
Printed by Lake Book Manufacturing

For Mom

CONTENTS

INTRODUCTION

EVER SEEN A BILLIONAIRE SMILE? I mean *really* smile, right up to the corners of their eyes, so you can tell they're not just mugging for the camera?

I haven't. In fact, it seems to me that the world's top earners tend to look haggard and pretty miserable. They've got all the resources and privileges in the world—access to things and experiences that we regular folks can only dream about—and yet they run around looking pissed off and stressed all the time. It's almost as if they accumulated their wealth with a business-is-hell mentality, constantly seeking to crush their competition, and now that the money's in the bank, they're exhausted. Either that or the sheer pressure of hanging on to all that money is giving them nonstop migraines.

But here's the thing: I'm worth tens of millions, and I smile *constantly*. I swear, if you ever meet me, you'll think, "This guy? In the flip-flops and T-shirt? With the shit-eating grin? *He's* a millionaire?"

I am. And unlike most high-profile millionaires, I use my wealth to enjoy my life. I mean, I focus on investing for the future and building stability for myself and my family, and I absolutely never throw my money away on luxury cars or obnoxious bling except when it is a reward for completing a project. But I also recognize that socking away cash just to have mountains of cash is . . . a little bit nuts. It's a socially acceptable form of hoarding, really. Especially if the process of accumulating more assets and money makes you feel strung out and tense.

Unless you're born rich, becoming a millionaire takes hard work, and lots of it. But that work shouldn't feel like a nonstop grind. And once you've achieved financial independence, you should *not* look like an anxiety-ridden zombie. You should build a life that allows you to wander the earth wearing flip-flops if that is what your heart desires. You should earn and accumulate wealth in ways that energize you instead of draining you.

I've been building wealth for decades, so I can attest that those things are possible. But I'll also warn you that, on top of all that hard work I mentioned earlier, you'll have to commit to a lifetime of learning. This is no one-and-done situation; it's a journey. A long one. I'm still on it myself.

Here's some proof: A few years back, I was looking for some established or retired rich people to interview. I wanted to soak up the wisdom of older wealthy people, talk with folks who were living the type of life that I wanted to live when I was seventy or eighty years old. Now, I don't know a ton of octogenarians, especially ones who maintain their net worth while traveling the globe, donating to worthy causes, and enjoying the good life. So I had to look outside my own natural friendship circles. Eventually, my search led to Chris Blackwell. (In case you haven't heard of him, he founded Island Records, is credited with popularizing reggae outside of Jamaica, and launched the careers of Bob Marley, Grace Jones, and U2. So, you know, he's a cool guy.)

Chris owns Goldeneye in Jamaica—the former estate of James Bond novelist Ian Fleming and now a luxury resort—and my family had rented there a few times in the past. So I sent Chris an email. I offered to donate a substantial sum to his favorite charity if he'd spend an hour with me, talking money and business advice. And I could not believe that he even answered. Most people do not. So I was doubly surprised when he said yes.

Allow me to geek out for a moment: I was thrilled to meet this man. I don't tend to get starstruck around musicians or movie stars, but this guy was the actual living embodiment of everything I wanted to be at eighty years old. He was smart, savvy, wealthy, artistic, well traveled, generous, interesting, and full of curiosity. And he came walking down the beach, barefoot in his swim trunks, and he was everything to me. I was like, "Oh my God, this is Chris Fucking Blackwell. And he owns this entire spectacular estate and the entire spectacular beach it's sitting on. How kick-ass is that?"

Eventually, we sat down to talk about my finances, and he said, "Did you really come down here for this?"

Like he couldn't believe I'd fly all the way to Jamaica and rent this house for several thousand dollars a night just to get financial advice from him for an hour. (And now that I write that out, I can see what he means because it sounds unusual.) At first, Chris seemed sure I was there to sell him something I hadn't pitched yet, but I wasn't. I was there to learn. And I'm at a stage in my life and investment career where I don't care what it costs to get the knowledge I need. I know that I simply won't get it if I don't seek it.

So I started sketching out my financial life on a cloth napkin at the bar. My wife, Sherri, was there with me, and we painted him a picture of our real estate holdings, stocks, investments, cash, the whole deal.

When I was just about done destroying the napkin with a Sharpie, he asked, "How do you think I can help you?"

Which, in itself, should have been a compliment. But it felt as if I was staring into the abyss.

So he followed up and asked, "You're already a very wealthy and accomplished man. What are you looking for?"

I blurted out, "How did you do this?" And I lifted my arms, gesturing around us. Because it looked to me as if he owned about half of the Jamaican coastline.

Then I asked, "How would I do this?"

And, my good people, he told me something that I've heard six times from three other mentors, but it blew my mind wide open coming from him. I needed to hear this particular advice from the lips of someone who was living my dream in order for it to sink in. And I'm gonna be that guy and make you wait until chapter eleven to hear the actual advice itself— but that's not even the point!

The point is that, even now, with millions in the bank, I am still learning. I seek advice and wisdom from mentors and do my best to model what they teach me. I will never feel like I know enough about finance or investment or market strategies. I will never rest on my accomplishments.

And neither should you.

Instead, you should plan on continuously learning about money and how you can make it work for you. You should envision the life you want in your heart of hearts and make a plan to build it.

That's how I got to where I am today. I never wanted to be the richest person in the world, but I wanted to travel and see the things I read about in *National Geographic*. I wanted financial freedom. I wanted to be able to do big, generous acts for the people I loved. All that adventure and philanthropy would be expensive, so I needed to find a way to make some serious money.

I did. And now I've got my dream life and a pretty freakin' impressive fortune, which I built over the years through strategy and hard work. I've made an agreement with myself to work for four years at a tech job, then take an entire year off for travel and learning. This allows me to have incredible experiences in long stretches, then go back to the industry I love once I'm rested and have once again found my passion. I've set insane, lofty goals for myself and have nailed most of them. I've met fantastic people, seen some of the most gorgeous places on Earth, and learned a wide array of skills from global masters. I dreamed the life I wanted, and then I built it, brick by brick.

You can, too. It won't be easy or fast, but if you enjoy challenging yourself, it will be fun. And I can teach you how to do it in a way that will set you up for security, happiness, wealth, and joy. Because the world's already got enough frowning, cutthroat, hypercompetitive billionaires.

Oh, before you turn the page, I should warn you that I'm from Texas, and this book will have stories from my life. Loads of them. It is my experience that storytelling is a way to both teach and capture the imagination. If you're looking for checklists and worksheets, or a dry instructional textbook, this ain't it. Though I will point you to simple and publicly available sources of information that I use every day.

I know full well that my experiences are just that: mine. But I also know that learning works a hell of a lot better when it isn't boring, gives readers emotional entry points, and offers lessons that the heart and mind can latch on to together. So, in the interest of helping you good people actually retain the knowledge I'm about to lay on you, there will be stories. No way around it.

Sound good? Are you ready to learn investment strategies to help you build wealth right now so you can retire early and enjoy life? Awesome. Let's do this.

CHAPTER
1

Why I Did It

LISTEN. I GREW UP WITH a schoolteacher single mother who went back to college at nearly thirty years old and worked two jobs most of her life. I got the message early: if we want more, we have to work more. My current net worth is in the tens of millions. And I'm here to tell you that you don't need to have money to make money.

I failed college math three times. I currently own dozens of investment properties and buy more every year. Making money is something anyone can do.

My first string of investments ended in bankruptcy. Since then I've sought advice and support from financially gifted people on a regular basis, getting help from people who are a hell of a lot smarter than I am. And I'm here to tell you that no one makes millions alone.

But first, I'm gonna tell you why I decided to get rich.

After serving in the US Air Force I moved to Austin, Texas, to use my veterans benefits to finish college. (Personal note: The military offers college benefits and even helps you buy a house. I often encourage young people to at least talk to a recruiter about all of the opportunities the military can provide.) I dedicated a lot of mental space to trying to figure out what I was going to do after graduation.

I'd been working various jobs since age twelve, so I knew that work would be part of the deal, but I also knew that I didn't want to just get a job. I wanted to find ways to make money that didn't involve trading dollars for hours, the way I'd seen my granddaddy do years before he invested a few spare bucks in oil wells. And, honestly, I didn't just want a job; I wanted security. I wanted flexibility and freedom. I was more than happy to work hard, but I wanted the work I did to lead to independence, not just to more work. So I schemed and researched and daydreamed.

I also eavesdropped a little.

Austin is a music town, and one of my college jobs was doing nighttime catering for *Austin City Limits* back when it was a small-potatoes TV show. (Yeah, I know. Sweet gig, right?) I got to meet many of my heroes in that six-and-a-half-year period. It was undeniably awesome. But I also got to spend a lot of time around artists and managers, and I began to surreptitiously tune in to some of their business conversations. You may have heard the cliché, "There is a *show* and there is a *business*." I got to see and hear some of it, and it was very interesting. (What? Catering gets boring. I couldn't help myself.)

I soon found out that in addition to making money on ticket sales and merch and album sales, musicians earned royalties every time a song was played on a radio station anywhere in the world. It was just pennies per play, but for a global hit with real staying power, that adds up over time. I also learned that musicians licensed their songs for use in commercials, movies, and TV, making yet more money off songs they may have written decades prior.

My granddaddy had talked about the idea of passive income when I was young, though he called it "mailbox money," since it involved getting royalty checks in the mail. He told me it meant doing research or work up front and getting paid over the long term. I knew that people earned passive income from investments such as dividend-yielding stocks and profits from their oil wells, but I'd never thought about the passive income side of the music industry before. If there were royalties to be earned off long-shelved records, there had to be other ways to earn passive income that I wasn't seeing.

Hello, I Hear You're Rich!

Being gregarious and a natural-born Texan, I began interviewing rich people. Basically, I asked my college buddies who around town was wealthy, set up some informational interviews, and picked the brains of a handful of Austin-based millionaires. Some of them were fancy people, some of them looked super average, and one looked like he earned less than I did as a broke college student.

His name was Tom, he was a regular at the restaurant where I worked and the brother of one of my professors, and he represented everything I love about Austin. He had long hair, was usually wearing cutoff shorts, and always had his dog with him and a beer in his hand. Total hippy, avid music lover—laid-back and happy. But it turned out he owned about 135 rental houses in Austin and was raking in the cash every month. Investing

in real estate had come up two or three times during my rich-people interviews, but Tom was the first guy who seemed to be a real expert on this
type of passive income.

I sat down with him one day, and I asked, "Tom, give me the truth.
Do you really make this money every day without even getting out of bed?"

"Yes, I do, but I have to pay all my bills first," he said. "Just because
somebody pays a thousand dollars a month in rent to live in one of my
houses, that doesn't mean I'm getting a thousand dollars a month from
each tenant. I have to watch my money very carefully and make sure all of
my bills get paid. Then whatever's left over is actually mine."

He took a pull of his beer.

"It's a long game, though. Because, over time, the mortgage gets paid
off by all that rent money. And all the equity that went into the mortgage
is mine to keep forever. Plus, once the mortgage is paid, then I actually do
get that thousand dollars every month."

If you read what Tom told me and thought, "Well, duh," then you are
way ahead of where I was then.

At the time, I could just barely grasp what he was saying. I could tell,
though, that he had deep knowledge about real estate, passive income,
and making smart investments. And since he hated monkey suits as much
as I did and led a low-profile, relaxed, truly independent life, I decided he
was the guy. He needed to be my mentor. Tom was the person to teach me
how to earn my mailbox money.

But when I asked him to show me the ropes, he flat-out refused.

"No way, man," he said. "I'm not your guy. I don't really fit the bill
for a millionaire, do I? I just take care of my properties, and I fish and I
water ski and I fix stuff that's broken. I don't get tied up in all that millionaire shit, and I don't think I have anything to teach you."

I knew he was wrong. He was a humble man who just didn't see himself as the mentor type, but he had so much knowledge and wisdom. And since I was stubborn, I kept hounding him.

"Just let me shadow you for a while," I begged. "I don't think you understand what I'm after here, Tom. All I wanna do is ride my mountain bike and own my own barbecue restaurant and have a bunch of rental houses and go tubing down the river. Oh, and chase a fresh crop of waitresses every semester. I want to do what you do. I want to *be* you, man."

He'd scratch at his stubble and look away. But he let me tag along a few times while he worked on his houses. And, eventually, Tom agreed to mentor me on an informal basis. In exchange for his input and guidance, I'd work one day a week fixing roofs or raking yards with him, lending a hand on whatever odd jobs he needed to tackle at his properties. He'd show me the ropes. It was education on the job—the best way to get it.

I expected Tom to talk endlessly about negotiation. Every real estate book I'd ever read was packed with advice on how to negotiate for the best price and avoid shady deals. But Tom wasn't a wheeler and dealer; he was an entrepreneur. He simply had a calculation for evaluating the financial health of a property. If the property price could fit that calculation, then he bought it. He taught me how to observe and run a business in a structured and calculated way.

I remember when I found the very first property I wanted to buy for myself and brought the deal to Tom for his input. I was so damned excited about the contract and thought we would talk about whether I got the right price for the house. And we sure as hell did not do that. Tom sat me down and said, "Okay, what do you think your maintenance costs are going to be on this property?"

I looked at him blankly.

"How about management costs? Don't manage that property yourself, Brady. Remember you wanna be an investor, a boss, a moneymaker. Let somebody else be a manager. That's not what you're trying to be when you grow up."

"I . . . uh . . ."

"Do you know how much rent you can get off this property?"

"I don't. I don't know, Tom," I said apologetically.

"That's okay, I'll teach you."

And he did. In an age long before Zillow, he showed me how to price a property in the market. He taught me to look at all the costs, including taxes, maintenance, management, and mortgage payments, and work backward from there. It was always nuts and bolts with Tom, God bless him, and this was his way of introducing me to a budget and teaching me about finance and operations. It was not sexy, but, damn, it was helpful.

Eventually, I started to realize that I wasn't going to be able to make serious money on one or two properties. I couldn't even do it with eight. Tom showed me that it was going to take twenty or more properties for me to live off my mailbox money, which was an overwhelming idea at first, but he encouraged me to pursue it. He gave me hope and a direction in which I could point myself.

"You can do this, too, Brady," Tom told me. "You can buy up and rent out houses right here in Austin."

Let me tell you, *that* excited me. Learning from Tom and getting that kind of encouragement from a man I respected lit a fire under me. I was going to be a real estate guy, too. I could feel it in my bones.

My First Big-Boy Money Goal

While he was mentoring me on real estate investment, Tom encouraged me to get serious about goal setting. He instructed me to read some books, do some research, put pen to paper, and commit to a solid number on a reasonable timeline.

"If you want to travel as much as you say you do, and still be a total music-head, and do it all on passive income streams, you need a plan. And you need it soon," he told me.

Now, here's the thing: Zig Ziglar, the legendary motivational speaker, was my Sunday school teacher. No kidding. When I was in high school, a couple friends and I would go out to his Sunday school classes in Dallas, just about every other week. He was so nice to us and even invited us over for lunch. And even though his books made little sense to me as a teenager, those classes were the first place anybody ever told me I needed a goal.

So, by the time Tom came around, I was an expert on goals. I'd been setting goals and crushing them since I was nineteen and joined the military to pay for college. But somehow I was struggling to set this big-picture, lifelong goal that Tom had asked me to set.

And here's why: I did what most humans do when they set goals. I imagined the thing I wanted to do, and when I didn't start making measurable, significant progress toward it right away, I started to beat myself up. I decided I was a failure.

Here's a little 20/20 hindsight on goal setting: When you set a new goal, remember that you're about to do something you've never done before. You're a rookie. And that's okay! But you should think of your goal as a direction or intention, not as a hard, bright line. Think to yourself,

"This is where I want to be. It's as far out as I can imagine, and I'm going to move toward it." But give that goal some fuzzy edges so you won't get mad or give up if you can't do everything perfectly on the first try.

Did you know that most of the planes taking off from the mainland United States for Hawaii take off in the wrong direction? Most runways go in every direction but east–west, so just to get started, pilots have to go in the wrong direction for a bit. But they know that, and they know they're going to have to course correct, and they know that course correction is a part of the journey.

Goals are the same. Plan to do things wrong, expect to stumble, know that you will have little failures along the way.

Your first money goal should be big, right? But the main reason it should be big is because that gets your imagination firing. It makes you start saying to yourself, "Well, if that's the finish line, how am I gonna get there?" It's a thinking exercise. It's a philosophy. Keep trying, failing, learning, and reorienting yourself in the direction of your goal.

I say this is advice from me to you, but Mr. Ziglar had a hand in it, too. He used to say something like, "When you first set a goal, set it for as far as you can see. And then once you get there, you will be able to see farther." You see why he made the big bucks? That's gold, right there. Keep moving toward those goals. If X doesn't work, don't give up; try Y. Or say to yourself, "Hey, I learned something new. Let's add that to the formula." Keep moving, keep investigating, keep trying, keep course correcting until you get there.

All right, that's enough advice for now. Let's get back to the main event: my story.

Since I didn't have any of the hindsight I just laid on you, I decided to seek goal-setting help from another expert. I got my hands on some Tony Robbins—the logical next step from Zig—and read up. I sat by the San

Marcos River trying to figure out what my life was going to be like. I was twenty-six, educated, driven, disciplined. The world was my goddamn oyster, but I was stumped.

This was especially true because the traditional route of college-grad-to-pencil-pusher held zero appeal to me. I'd done a stint in the military before I hit college, and I never really thought I was going to fit into the corporate world. I assumed that corporate life would be a lot like the military: wearing a certain uniform every day, suppressing my individuality, sticking to someone else's schedule, and never getting the flexibility I craved. I'd never held a corporate job in my life, but those negative assumptions steered me away from the cube farm.

Once my dreams and desires finally started to gel, I landed on a pretty pie-in-the-sky goal. I decided I wanted to make $10,000 every month without working, and I wanted that to be happening regularly by the time I was thirty-six. I pulled that number directly out of thin air, but it seemed like a good goal, and when I talked with Tom about my new goal, he seemed impressed. So I committed.

And since my mentor was a real estate whiz who believed I could follow in his footsteps, I decided I'd start by buying a few properties.

Brady Booms, Then Busts

It's worth saying that the first house I bought wasn't the one I'd envisioned. In my mind, my first house was going to be a brand-new, shiny, spotless house that I'd move into myself. In my hilariously misguided twenty-five-year-old mind, somebody was going to have a brand-new, shiny, spotless house with zero maintenance issues that they'd owner-finance to me for no money down.

Funny, right? I think so, too, now that I know better. As you might've guessed, my first house was anything but new and shiny. Here's what happened.

Everybody who went to school with me knew I was trying to interview millionaires. They knew it because I talked about it all the time, to anyone who'd listen. So one day a classmate flagged me down and said, "Hey, you might want to talk to my granddad."

"Oh, great!" I said. "Does he own a bunch of houses?"

"Nope," he said. "But he owns a house over on the golf course that's sitting empty. I've been living there awhile myself, but now he's looking to sell it. Cheap."

He went on to explain that his granddad had bought what he thought would be his retirement home on the golf course community, but then plans changed. He and his wife decided to spend their summers in Nevada on Lake Tahoe and their winters here in Texas. So they moved back and forth between those two towns for six years, then the wife passed away while they were in Nevada.

"Granddad decided he was never going back to Texas again," my pal told me. "Said he never did like that house anyway."

The house was sitting empty, and the grandson started living there while he was going to college. Sounds fine so far, but here's the kicker. The golf course had filed for bankruptcy. The grass was knee-high everywhere, and the place was in total disrepair. As for the house itself, the air conditioner was busted, and there was a gaping hole in the roof. Oh, and a family of raccoons had moved in. No lie. Plus the trash hadn't been collected in ages and the whole place stank to high heaven.

Despite the red flags, I decided this was my shot at buying a house. I talked to his granddad, who was a fine gent and immediately offered me this deal.

"Tell you what I'll do," he said. "If you'll start making me a payment, I will sell the house to you right now, no money down. I want it paid off in ten years, so we'll need to set an amortization schedule."

I wasn't 100 percent sure what that meant, but I went to Tom and explained the situation, and he took me to a local attorney who charged $100 to write up a simple contract for owner-financing. Which I signed.

And then my pal's granddad said to me, "If you ever miss one payment, I'm taking my house back."

I gulped. I shook his hand. And then I was a property owner.

A roommate helped me patch up the roof, and my college buddies helped me rip out the moldy carpeting. I got the raccoons out and fixed up the water heater when it quit working. I rented two of the bedrooms to classmates and moved myself into the other one. It was a run-down central Texas house, with no air-conditioning and a concrete floor, but it was mine.

And you can bet your ass that once I saved up enough money to replace the carpet and get the house in decent shape, I moved out. That's right, I rented all three bedrooms to other guys and moved across town to a nicer place. And just like that, I was a landlord.

The market was ripe at that time, so I kept working the owner-financed no-money-down angle and buying up houses as fast as I could reasonably afford to. Once I had one or two rental properties under my belt, I found out that a friend of mine from college was a property manager. (We'll get into why I wanted to acquire but not manage my own properties later.) His name was Ben, and the two of us decided to team up on buying houses. I'd scope the deals and handle the sales and he would manage them.

Ben soon found a run-down duplex near a university that we lease-purchased (a lease-purchase agreement allows you to rent until you pay off the property). We began to refurbish it. One day we had an idea over lunch that we should approach all of the homeowners on the street with the lease-purchase or owner-financed opportunity. And the idea worked way beyond our expectations. Within twelve months, we had purchased eight duplexes, or sixteen units.

We bought as many properties as we could in a year and a half with no money down. This was in the 1990s, when Austin was still up-and-coming, so our average down payment on a house was less than $1,800. By the end of that eighteen months, we had twenty-eight units and were up to our eyeballs in debt. And it gets worse.

Ben had been getting credit card offers like I had never seen. It actually became a running joke. I was still waiting tables at night and scrambling for every dollar and, rightfully, no one was going to offer me a credit card. But Ben couldn't open the envelopes fast enough. And that's when the trouble began.

We had a good business model and a great team. What we did not have was enough experience or financial education.

Since we were cash poor and many of our houses were serious fixer-uppers, we figured we could borrow money off the credit cards to make improvements because we'd soon have enough money from rent income to pay them off. We could even borrow for a few of the down payments we'd skipped. Once we refinanced—which we figured was about twenty-four months away for each property—we'd pay off remaining balances for good.

Sounds like a decent plan, right? Unfortunately, we had no idea about compound interest, no clue that the debt we were racking up would slowly but surely grow if we couldn't pay it down fast. On top of that, Ben was forgoing salary to help our business and needed to use these cards for some of his personal expenses. I was still waiting tables and using that income to deal with my own rent, food, gas, and other expenses. We were living for the payoff that would surely come. But it didn't.

After about two years, it all imploded. Ben's credit card debt was over $100,000. He was only twenty-five.

Since we had purchased every property with no money down, no credit company would ever find our holdings. They were all purchased using promissory notes. (Hold tight, I'll give you tons on this topic in chapter seven.) Since none of those deals would show up on a credit report, it did go through our heads that Ben could file for bankruptcy and we could keep the properties. At one point, I even told him he could file for bankruptcy and I could sell his half of the business back for a dollar. I've since learned that's total bullshit. Let me restate that for emphasis: That idea would never have worked. The IRS has seen that sort of scheme before and I do not believe it would have worked. But I was desperate to save what Ben and I had done together and I knew that they might be his credit cards but I was just as responsible for this mess. Eventually, we realized we had to face the music. Ben filed for bankruptcy, and it was terrible. Just terrible. We were best friends, and I knew I was just as guilty of mismanagement and wrongheadedness as he was. But the credit cards were all in his name, and the debt was technically his. So it was his name that got dragged through the mud.

The bankruptcy court dissolved our little organization, and all of Ben's assets went to the US government. However, the court decided to let me keep a few of the properties we'd bought. Ben wanted a break from the ordeal and started looking at MBA programs and a way to turn this tough lesson into a positive. I kept a few of the houses and got a boatload of guilt to go with them.

I lost my best friend. I couldn't eat and dropped twenty pounds in about a month. It was one of the lowest points of my entire life.

It was also when I learned that working a second job could save my ass.

Another close friend of mine saw me hurting and told me I could take a room at his house, as long as I kept working two jobs: catering and investing. He told me, "You're not a slacker, you're just a guy with bad luck. If you keep up your work ethic, I believe you'll make it." I was so grateful to him and so happy to hear he still believed in me. I was the world's best roommate, always quiet and courteous, making sure he barely knew I was there.

But I was miserable. About a year later, I was still working forty to fifty hours per week at the restaurant and trying to keep these houses together in my free time. With Ben gone, I had to do the property management myself, and it was time-consuming, exhausting work. Plus, every time I went down to one of the rentals, all I could think of was Ben and how our pipe dream had turned into a pipe bomb. It felt like the whole thing exploded in his face and left me untouched. (Well, mostly.)

One afternoon, I just couldn't stand it anymore. I was skinny, depressed, exhausted, and just about at the end of my rope. I remember carrying a paint bucket, walking down the street to paint one of my houses all by myself, and knowing I was going to have to sleep there that night. No air-conditioning, beat-up wood floor, no furniture. That didn't bother me, really, but the rest of the situation was slowly killing me from the inside. I was just crying, carrying this paint bucket down the goddamn street, thinking, "Soon enough, I'm going to have to file for bankruptcy, too. I just don't know when."

Money Mentor #2 Appears

What I also didn't know is that the bankruptcy court had left me with the properties that actually made money. They repossessed the duds for the government to auction off and did me a favor by releasing the gems back to me. I was down to about six houses, but they were the good ones.

This is the start of me getting deadly serious about how finances worked. The bankruptcy attorney expressed it to me very well. He said that he was giving me the best cash-flowing properties but that he was concerned that I did not know how to evaluate a cash-flow. He said that if I did not get a financial education, I may well be back in his office again. His concern was a warning: learn how to run a business, not just acquire properties.

Still, I was overwhelmed and lost. The court was holding my properties but not paying their mortgages, which is a common practice when bankruptcy comes into play. I was legally on the hook for those mortgage payments myself, but no longer owned the houses and couldn't collect the rent. So I sure as shit couldn't pay the mortgage. I was getting calls from banks and creditors asking for their money, and I had no idea what to do. I was living between a rock and a hard place.

One day after work, I took a six-pack of beer from the fridge at the restaurant, put it in a cooler, and went over to the office of the bankruptcy court appointee. I sat in this attorney's lobby, cracked a beer, and thought to myself, "I'm either going to finish this beer, or Ron is going to see me."

Ron saw me.

I went into his office, and I remember sitting there, head in my hands, saying, "Look, man, if you think I have anything else, I don't. No rabbit is gonna come out of this hat. I've got nothing. And if you keep holding these properties, and you keep not paying the bills, I'm going to lose everything. Everything."

I took a shaky breath and said, "So, you can either tell me how I'm going to get out of this and never go bankrupt again, or I'm going to drink all this beer and just sit here and cry."

"Hand me one of those beers," he said. He took a long pull. "So you don't have anything else?"

I said, "No, sir, I don't have shit. I've got a GI bill and a barbecue job, and that's who I am."

"How did you guys acquire all this property in this short time? Is there someone else with you?" Ron asked, incredulous.

"No, we just didn't know you couldn't!" I said. "A friend was giving me advice. I was buying up all the houses I could find, and my buddy was managing the properties. We borrowed some money off credit cards, but we didn't know how the interest would compound. So we just got in over our heads without understanding what we were doing."

He paused for a long moment. Then he said, "All right. I'm going to tell you how to stay out of bankruptcy court. But lawyers don't usually give free advice, so listen closely."

"The first bill you pay is the taxman's," Ron told me. "Everybody who ends up in my office has pretty much the same story. They didn't save enough for the taxman, because they thought the taxman could wait. That's as backward as it can be. In a jam, the taxman gets paid first, and everyone else can hang tight."

He looked at his watch. Took a swig from the beer he was drinking before continuing.

"What you've done here is really unique and extraordinary, with all this owner-financing stuff. And it's clear you've got a knack for scouting good deals. But you're going to need real lending sources going forward. Why don't you go talk to a banker?" Ron said. "I can help you find a lawyer for setting up a business entity, but you need input on your money matters, too. And you need it from someone who knows what they're talking about."

I told him I didn't know any bankers, so he gave me the name of one he knew in town named Frank. I told Frank the nuts and bolts of my situation, and he said, "Man, you're not the first one. Now let me see what I can make out of this."

And he proceeded to work his banker magic on my catastrophe of a financial situation. This banker "magic" is more commonly known as accounting, but it was new to me. Two or three of the promissory notes were paid down enough that he could refinance some—but not all—of them, and not immediately. Still, it was with his help that I started crawling out of the hellhole my life had become.

The Moral of the Story Is . . .

As you've probably guessed, things got better for me. A lot better. However, I firmly believe that hitting rock bottom is what made my current success possible. I learned that investing without understanding is insane. I learned that just because you can do something, it doesn't mean you should. But the three most important things I learned are as follows:

1. **Pay for good advice:** Do not—I repeat, *do not*—start investing without getting paid advice from an expert. A lawyer, a financial adviser, a banker, someone who knows so much about investing they could do it in their sleep. Get yourself a mentor before you hand over any money or sign any contracts.

2. **Think hard and ask good questions:** Once you've found your mentor, don't waste their time. Research your area of interest on your own, take notes, and formulate questions before you meet. Don't ask for facts; ask for guidance instead. And be prepared to hear things you don't want to hear.

3. **Assemble a team:** The myth of the self-made man is absolute bullshit. You will not make a fortune by yourself because no one ever has. In addition to your mentor, consider finding people who will invest with you, peers who are also fascinated by your area of interest, experts, professors, and teachers—anyone who is smart and passionate and willing to help you.

I learned these three lessons the hard way. I considered giving up on investing forever, and I definitely had moments where I found myself thinking, "Maybe I should abandon ship and get a real job. Maybe the cube farm *is* the place for me, after all."

But then I asked myself, "What about that goal? Do you still want to bring in $10K every month without working? Is that still the dream, still the ultimate outcome you want for yourself?"

And the answer was yes. That was my ideal future, even after all the pain and loss that my first crack at investing had caused me. Over time I would see that setbacks of all shapes and sizes are totally normal; in fact, without them we have a much harder time learning. Failure doesn't just keep us humble, it keeps us sharp. And it makes us resilient. After we learn how much it sucks to fall down, we learn how fantastic it feels to pull ourselves back up again.

Of course, I had some incredible people who showed up for me whenever I fell down, who reached out their hands to pull me up off the hard dirt floor. I got lots of encouragement from role models and mentors, some of whom you've just met and many of whom you're yet to meet. I had a team. And without them, I might not have kept going. Without them, I might've abandoned my dream, resigned myself to an office life, and never made millions.

But like I said, I'm from Texas. I'm stubborn and tough and ridiculously enthusiastic about the things that fire me up. So I kept going, and you know what? I hit that goal. By age thirty-six, I was bringing in $10K every month on passive income revenue alone. The money was in the mailbox.

So I set a new goal. And if you'll kindly continue on to chapter two, we'll talk more about setting and crushing your own financial goals.

CHAPTER
2

"Rich" Is Not a Goal

Since I plan to get good and controversial in every single chapter of this book, let's get that party started right now: I do not want you to be rich.

I do not want your goals to include getting rich or living like a rich person, or anything that involves the word *rich* at all, ever. And I say this, gentle reader, for the simple reason that rich is just not specific enough. It's so vague that it's practically meaningless. *Rich*, like *middle-class*, is an overused and under-defined term that really just comes down to how you feel about yourself. Or how you compare yourself to other people.

We all do a lot of comparing these days, since we're living in the golden age of social media. (Yeah, I'm gonna go there. Brace yourselves.) Log on to Instagram and you'll see the world's love-hate relationship with rich writ large—mainly when someone posts photos showing designer outfits and flashy jewelry, then gets roasted in their own comment section.

Open your Spotify account and you'll hear mainstream artists singing about cash money, crazy spending, massive diamonds, and gold grills. They'll list their favorite designer names and fancy cars, tell you how amazing it feels to be rich, and do their best to stir up a little jealousy. Hearing those big, bold brags can be entertaining, but buying into the "live big, spend big" philosophy is just plain foolish. And so is setting your sights on getting rich as a financial goal.

I'll tell you right now that no accountant or financial adviser in the universe would sign off on a goal as vague as "I want to be rich." They'd demand something that's more dialed-in, more precise. And to my knowledge no Fortune 500 or publicly traded company has ever set a quarterly goal of getting rich. Instead, they stick to measurable outcomes like, "We will have total sales of $100 million this fiscal year." See the difference? $100 million is measurable. It's concrete, which makes it easier to build milestones that'll get you there. We know if we have $25 million in sales by March, then we have $75 million to go. Optimistically, if we have $105 million in sales by October, we can take it easy since we've exceeded our goal.

You may have picked up this book because you want to be rich, and that's fine to get started thinking into your future. But this chapter is our financial goal-setting chapter, and I'm going to force you to define yours more specifically than that. Rich is not the result or outcome of a measurable plan. Rich is not a goal.

So we're going to focus on goals that can be clearly defined. That'll help us know how far away those goals are right now and how to recognize them when we get there. Later in the chapter, we'll dig into how you can set your own personal goal (or goals) around wealth building, but before we do that, let's set a group goal. Are you ready?

You want to have access to more money than you've got right now, regularly, for a really long time, right? For the purposes of this book, I am going to call that being financially independent. And because it's my ship and I make the rules, I'll say that being financially independent encompasses the amount of passive income you'll need to cover your monthly bills on a regular basis, for multiple years at a time. That's where we'll start. I think we can all agree that if you don't have to worry about your bills for the foreseeable future, you're already rich and have learned skills that will make you even richer. Right?

Nod your head and say, "Yes, Brady." Good.

Oh, and one more thing. Depending on the cost of living where you are, you may not need as much passive income as other people to achieve financial independence. This is good news! But it also means you should not compare yourself to people who aren't on your corner of the map.

Want an example? I have a home on the beach in Del Mar, California, and another home in Austin, Texas. If we compare the cost of living statistics for both of those areas, we'll see they're wildly different. At the time of printing, the US Bureau of Labor Statistics reports that the cost of living in Del Mar is 300 percent higher than in Austin, so to reach financial independence in Del Mar, you'll need to bring in a hell of a lot more money than you would living in Austin.

(And now a word from our accountants, lawyers, and socioeconomic statisticians: SoCal does have a robust job market that includes high-paying industries like biotech, so I'm not saying it's impossible to live there and be a financially independent person. My point is that we've got to consider individual circumstances and environmental factors versus having a one-size-fits-all approach to financial independence. Terms and conditions apply, blah blah, etc.)

Bottom line: If all you're after are status and flash, close this book right now. If you're unable to imagine a goal more concrete than "get rich," you can finish your beer and go home. But if you're ready to get specific, build a plan, and set it in motion, you've come to the right place.

Invisible Wealth and Real Independence

I wanted to write this book because I had the unfair advantage of an amazing financial education. The people in my life bent over backward to make sure I understood the basics of earning, saving, and investing—from the time I was very young.

When I was about eleven years old, my granddaddy took me to a Dallas Cowboys football game. At that time, the tickets would've been a huge expense for him, so this was definitely a special occasion—not something we got to do together very often. So we're sitting there, taking in the pageantry, the colors, the crowd noise, and it was overwhelming for me as a kid from a tiny little Texas town, right? I mean, I knew what football was, but seeing a game in person felt downright magical. I can't remember at what point in the game my granddaddy started talking dollar signs, but I remember we had hot dogs in our hands and were chowing down.

Then he said, "Brady, who do you think is the richest person in this entire stadium?"

And I said, "Well, Papa, that's easy. It's Roger Staubach, the quarterback!"

"I understand why you'd think like that. Those guys make a lot of money," he said. "But you're wrong. Look up there, in that skybox."

He pointed a gnarled finger across the field, at a glassed-in private box over the 50-yard line.

"You see that one man up there? In the gray suit? That's Clint Murchison, Jr., the man who owns the entire Cowboys team."

"Okay," I said.

"That's the man who writes Roger Staubach's paycheck. He's the richest man in this building. In fact, I do believe he's the richest man in the state! It's not always the star who's making serious money. More often, it's the person who pays the star's check. It's the person who built the business, the person who put in the extra time, the person who said, 'I'm not doing this for the attention or the perks. I'm doing it for the independence.' You understand?"

Well, kinda, but at age eleven I was too young to realize he was trying to impart wisdom through his stories. Still, I remembered his words for many years afterward, and they shaped my views on wealth and the value of independence.

That story is the reason I'm asking you readers to focus on the idea of being financially independent instead of rich. The old cliché says "money is power," but if you ask me, what we're really trying to get at is independence. We don't want to lord our wealth over other people to feel powerful; what in hell would be the point of that? We want to worry less and enjoy life more. We want to feel secure and stable. We want to dive into work when we need to work, and relax when we don't instead of feeling like we have to keep running on the hamster wheel until we're dead.

Wealth doesn't need to be conspicuous; it just needs to support us. And in order to accumulate enough of it to be properly supported, we'll need to do some careful planning and a little bit of math.

All Goals Must Be Specific and Time Sensitive

Did I say this already? I did. I'm going to take a moment and say it again on the off chance you've been skimming: no vague goals.

When you start training for a triathlon, you don't think to your-self, "I should probably be a better runner." When you decide to build a house, you don't think to yourself, "I'd like to finish this house someday and have it cost a reasonable amount of money." You get specific! You set incremental goals along the way. You figure out what resources you'll need, you create a timeline, and you get to work.

An easy way to kick off that process is to start with a desired outcome and plan backward. Envision a huge goal and set smaller goals that move you toward it. Set your own financial goals like a corporation would: choose a figure you want to hit, then build steps that lead to it. Decide how much you want in the bank, or how much you want to bring in each year, then figure out how you'll do it.

Remember what Tom taught me about figuring out what to charge tenants for rent? How I needed to look at all the costs, including taxes and maintenance, management and mortgage payments, and work backward from there? It's the same concept, applied to your own financial goals.

Think about the early days of NASA and the United States setting a goal of putting a man on the moon. It's the mid-1960s and nobody had even built a rocket ship at that point, let alone put a person into orbit. The engineers and astronauts did not write "MOON OR BUST" on their fore-heads with Sharpies and focus on that one single goal. They made the moon

"RICH" IS NOT A GOAL   33

the big goal and created a ladder of smaller goals that would move them toward the big goal. Eventually. And with several misfires along the way.

They set a fuzzy-line intention to make everyone ask themselves, "How would we do that?" And the engineers and scientists and everybody else came in and said, "Well, for starters, we'd have to find some sort of a booster that would get us out of the Earth's orbit." And somebody else said, "And we'll have to create a suit that allows people to breathe in space." (Of course, that's an oversimplification. Bear with me, people.)

Yet, over time, they cobbled these related ideas together. Then there were a couple of dry runs. There were a couple of failed orbits, and some successful ones. And finally, in July 1969, Apollo 11 touched down, and Neil Armstrong jumped into all that moon dust and made history. But it took years. And it took backward planning and dozens of smaller, incremental goals to get there.

Want an example from the financial world? Try this on for size.

Say you want to have $1 million in cash in the bank. It's a nice big goal, and it's attached to a specific number. That means you'll know for certain when you've achieved it and can commence patting yourself on the back. But as a goal, it's still way too vague.

Accumulating wealth is a long game, so consider time as a key factor. When do you want to have $1 million in cash in the bank? By the time you're thirty-five? Within the next ten years? Give yourself enough time to learn and master the strategies you'll use to make this money. And that means years, not months, my friends. Don't rush it. But do include both a number ($1 million in cash) and a time frame (by the time I'm thirty-five). That gives you two concrete guardrails to work with as you plan your incremental goals.

How to Select Your First Big Financial Goal

Remember that when I set my goal of making $10,000 per month without working, I pulled that number from thin air. No research, no reasoning, just a random number that sounded mighty fine to a twenty-six-year-old living it up in the '90s. And that's okay! Because most people have zero financial goals, setting any goals at all puts you ahead of the curve.

However, you can be a little more strategic about setting your own goals, if you want. The best way I've found is to think about the *why* that's driving you. Why do you want to have more money? Why do you want a higher monthly income, or a big chunk of change sitting in the bank? If you can steer away from feelings and toward activities, all the better. Here's why: Our brains can get easily wrapped up in the size and scope of the goal such that it looks impossible. To combat this natural reaction, we can give the brain a small piece of the total goal to focus on. Once the small chunk is completed, we start working on the next small chunk.

Say you want more money so you can travel more often. Break that down into bite-sized chunks. Do you want to take two international trips per year and another four domestic trips? Make a list of ideal destinations, then focus on the most expensive ones to build in some padding on your estimates. Let's say Japan for your international trip and San Francisco for domestic.

1. Pick a time of year you might go and the length of time you'd stay.
2. Look up flight prices.

3. Research hotels in the cities or regions you'd visit.

4. Investigate the costs of eating out, transit, and entertainment.

5. Figure in any associated costs, like pet sitters, or unpaid time off from your job.

6. Total it all up.

Let's say you figure you'll need roughly $7,000 for a week in Japan and $1,500 for a four-day stay in San Francisco. Multiply by the number of trips you want to take each year, and you'll get $14,000 for international travel and $6,000 for domestic. That's an estimated $20,000 total for annual travel. (Since these are your highest-priced destinations, you might not need so much, but it's better to plan for higher costs than lower ones.)

Now! This is not a one-shot deal; this is a long-term commitment. You're envisioning a life for yourself that includes $20,000 of travel every single year. Hopefully, you're already making some money every year. Your task is to decide how you'll earn that extra twenty-large. (No clue? Chapters three to five are chock-full of ideas and advice. We'll get there soon.)

Don't care about travel, but want to own a boat? Research boat prices, dock fees, maintenance costs, and all of the expenses associated with boat ownership. Estimate high and tack the number onto your annual income goal.

Don't care about boats but want to live on a hobby farm? Or collect tons of art? Or build a cutting-edge recording studio in your home? Every dream comes with a to-do list, an assload of research, and a budget. Investigate all the costs, risks, and expenses you can find. Add them up, multiply, and step back.

Boom. You've just set a financial goal. Commence the back patting.

If your financial *why* is less concrete, this gets harder—though not impossible. If your answer to "Why do you want to have more money?" is, "I want to feel more secure," or "So I can stop worrying about my bank balance all the damned time," you'll need other guardrails. You can't really research costs and expenses around reducing anxiety. Luckily, I've got a workaround for you.

If Your Goal Is Financial Independence . . .

I flatly refuse to help you get rich, but I desperately want to help you become financially independent. And as far as I can tell, being financially independent covers most of the vague financial whys that consume people. It reduces worry, it increases security, it allows us to truly enjoy our lives. It's the secret sauce, my people, and I fully support it as your brand-spanking-new financial goal.

How do you get there? Same way: work backward.

1. If you want to own your own home, figure out what your mortgage, utilities, and taxes will be in your hometown each month. If you plan to be a lifetime renter, total up your rent and utilities.
2. Calculate your monthly living expenses, including car payments, gas, food, entertainment, loans, and anything else. (Already using a personal monthly budget? You've got this stuff covered. No idea how to create a personal monthly budget? Apps like EveryDollar and Mint can help.)
3. If possible, track down your living expenses for the past three or four months and average them. If you bank online, it should be relatively easy to find and total up your recent expenditures.

If you have enough passive income to pay for housing and living expenses every month, your nonnegotiables are covered. You are financially independent. If you want to invest or travel, or do anything besides hang out at home and eat the occasional sandwich, you will need additional income, likely from a job of some sort. But as long as your basic bills are paid by passive income, that's it. You're financially independent.

If Your Goal Is a Number . . .

Say that, like me, you've got your heart set on $10,000 a month without working. Or that you're aiming for the goal we discussed earlier in the chapter, "$1 million in cash in the bank by age thirty-five." How do you work backward toward that goal?

The bad news is that I don't have an easy answer to that one.

The good news is that your money mentor can help.

What's that, now? You don't have a mentor? I think you mean, "I don't have a mentor yet."

Because if you're aiming for $10K in passive income every month, it's time for you to seek and ask for outside input and guidance. You need help that's specific to your goals and your interests from someone who's achieved similar things. You need someone who knows how passive income is regulated in your state, someone who has earned it for years, someone who is willing to tutor you directly and help out when things go sideways. (Which they inevitably will. That's a promise.) If your money goals are based on hitting certain numbers by certain times, you will need support. And a mentor is the absolute best source of financial support.

Of course, there are also seminars, internet research, books, and internships. You can find ways to hang out around wealthy people, observe them, find out how they did it, learn by osmosis. But I still think a mentor (or two or three) will be a better bet. A mentor has done what you want to do already, so their advice will be tailored to your goals and needs. A mentor can answer your questions directly and succinctly. A mentor can help you course correct.

A good money mentor will also be your cheerleader and your voice of reason. Whenever you do that all-too-human thing of getting in your own way, your mentor will remind you that you only need to be directionally correct. You don't need to know everything; you just need to know enough to get started.

Speaking of which . . .

Get Started *Now*

Here's an autobiographical tidbit that might surprise you: I work in—and love—corporate America. Big tech, specifically. That's right, folks, I have made millions in passive income, but I also hold down a day job. We'll talk more about that in chapter three, but here's why I'm telling you now: Working corporate jobs has taught me that if you know 70 to 80 percent of what you need to know, you know enough to get started. You do not need to see the whole landscape or anticipate every roadblock. You just need to have a solid idea, and you can proceed from there.

Let's take the iPhone. That thing changed the world, as everybody knows. Do you think the design team knew every single detail about building the iPhone when they got started? Hell no, they didn't. They knew that they wanted to create a phone that would play music and connect you to the internet and that they were smart enough to do it. So—just like the NASA teams—they started setting incremental goals and chipping away at them. They didn't sit on their hands until they'd gathered every bit of research they could; they dove right in! They worked on one aspect of the machine at a time, course corrected as they learned, and added new knowledge as they progressed.

If Apple had tried to understand every niggling little aspect of creating the iPhone before they launched the design-and-build process, some other company would've beat them to it. They knew about 70 to 80 percent of what it would take. And they trusted themselves.

People are too hung up on having an absolute formula; they're afraid that anything short of total certainty will lead to failure. But the truth is that most entrepreneurs, millionaires, and wildly successful humans do not know the absolute formula. Mainly because there is no absolute formula. Smart, financially independent people gather as much knowledge as they can, and they behave in ways that they believe are directionally correct.

That's a term I learned in the corporate world. *Directionally correct* means, "Do we have enough solid information and confidence in our idea to move forward?" Multibillion-dollar companies don't wait until they know everything to get started, and you shouldn't either. For two huge reasons:

1. **You'll start looking for "no":** If you look hard enough, you'll always find a reason not to do something. And researching the living daylights out of a personal goal will lead you down the rabbit hole of possible failures.

2. **You'll wait too long:** There's a saying in real estate that I love: "The best time to buy was twenty years ago. The second best time is now." You can wait forever for the right signals or factors or for the stars to align. Don't. When it comes to money, doing absolutely anything right away is better than doing the right thing later on.

Earning enough passive income to cover your living expenses is a simple goal, but it's one that will take some hard work and a long-ass time to reach. In fact, you are not going to become financially independent this year. Or next year. Or possibly in the next five years. Tony Robbins has said that people tend to overestimate what they can do in one year, and they tend to underestimate what they can do in ten years. Start planning for and acting on your financial goals right now so you can get closer to achieving them on a reasonable timeline.

And if you're getting all mopey at the thought of tackling a goal that will take years to achieve, consider this: doing it this way sets you up to do it forever. You'll have the skills, the knowledge, and the endurance to be a lifelong moneymaker. You'll be a cross-country runner instead of a sprinter. Which means financial independence forever, not just for now.

Four Years of Work, One Year of Travel

Welcome to the Brady Practices What He Preaches Edition.

I never thought I'd find a traditional office job I actually enjoyed. I believed I was way too stubborn and independent to sit at a gray desk under fluorescent lights. So imagine my shock when I landed a job in technology and discovered I was good at it and that I adored it. I worked my way up to an international career with some of the world's largest and coolest companies, even though doing that was never part of my plan. My plan, you'll remember, was to make $10,000 a month without working and live out my Austin hippie dream, complete with concerts and tubing down rivers and lots of adventure travel. And even when I jumped on the tech bandwagon and found myself unexpectedly enjoying the ride, I always assumed I'd come back to that freewheeling artistic life. It never was even a question.

The salaries from my tech jobs enabled me to pay for more than just my living expenses and save a good amount on top of that, moving me closer to financial freedom. But those jobs also complicated my dreams. If I was going to visit all of the great museums of Europe—and do it right, not just on weekend-long trips—that was going to require time. If I was going to climb mountains, I'd need about three weeks of PTO per mountain. If I was going to see all the concerts I really wanted to see, including in gorgeous cities far from Austin, I was going to need even more time away from my desk.

Eventually I realized that my $10,000 a month could be used to buy back my time. I realized that my original bargain with myself wasn't just about the money, it was about time and freedom. I decided to work really hard for ten years, or however long it took until I had enough leverage and flexibility to buy my life back—a life with travel and concerts and flip-flops on the beach.

So when I finally did hit that first big goal of $10,000 a month in passive income, the question became, "Am I actually going to do this? Am I going to give up a successful global career and buy my life back, like I've always planned to do?"

Even though it was fully possible, the idea scared the pants off me. I'd have to give up something that was really working—my technology career—in order to reclaim my original dream. I'd always thought that walking away from tech was going to be the easiest decision I'd ever make. In my imagination, I'd hit $10K a month, waltz into my office, and say, "Fuck this shit. I'm going to go work at the barbecue restaurant. I'm going to ride my mountain bike around town and then jet off to Jamaica. So long, suckers!"

But it wasn't like that at all. It was incredibly hard to convince myself that walking away was the right choice. I was doing work that I loved, work that kept me intellectually stimulated, work that was helping me earn above and beyond my self-set goals. Bailing felt downright stupid.

And at the same time, I knew that if I didn't keep the promise I'd made to myself, I'd regret it. Seeing art, traveling the world, learning new things, challenging myself physically, pursuing true adventure—those were my passions. I had to actually do those things, or my life would feel hollow and brittle. And on top of that, if I didn't quit working for some period of time and really indulge my inner hippie, I'd have no idea who I really was. Everything I'd believed about myself for the past fourteen years would be a lie. I had to go live those artistic lives or I wouldn't be living my own truth.

So! I talked to a trusted money mentor, and here's the deal we struck: I would take off a nice big chunk of time, make a list of all the amazing things I was going to do during that time, and spend it checking items off the list. When that agreed-upon period of time was up, I'd go back to work. Back to my big-boy job, with a desk and a salary and all that regular-guy stuff.

I was able to make this new deal with myself because I realized my own personal brand of abundance encompassed more than just money. It was a network of people that I knew in technology and finance, a strong network I'd built over many years. It was a top-notch education. It was an impressive resume that included stints with two of the world's most respected technology companies. I decided to trust that all that nonmonetary abundance I'd cultivated would support me when I was ready to come back from Bora Bora or wherever.

But let me tell you, it was not easy. I sat at the kitchen table with my girlfriend, now my wife, and agonized. I doubted myself. I had endless stress nightmares. It was one of the scariest things I've ever done. I was not woohooing my way out the door while giving everybody the finger. I felt like I was putting my feet on the thin, translucent surface of a frozen pond and hearing it crack. Every step triggered a new crack, and every new crack made it feel like I was going to fall through.

But I knew what my dream was. So I committed to taking a whole year off from working.

Before embarking on this crazy year-off experiment, I sent out an email to about thirty friends, asking, "If I told you that I was taking one year off, and that I could not work during that year, what could you see me doing?" For the most part, their replies fell into one of three buckets: art, education, and travel. (This confirmed what I knew about myself and thought I really wanted to do anyway. Bonus.)

Armed with that knowledge, I started making a to-do list for everything I wanted to do, see, and accomplish during my year off work. The list started with cooking, diving, and learning a new language. Once I was officially off the clock, the first thing I did was take fifteen hours of cooking classes at Le Cordon Bleu. (Harder than you'd think, people. And as fun as it was, I am still a lousy cook.) After never scuba diving a single day in my life, I committed to getting certified as a rescue diver in St. Barts. And then I hired a French coach and went to Berlitz for three months.

And as I was soaking up the sun on somebody's massive yacht, taking diving breaks to peep at the fish, speaking kind-of-but-not-even-close

French, drinking champagne, and doing everything most people only dream of, that's when I knew, "Okay, this year is worth it."

Sometime during those first months off, I got two incredible phone calls. One was from Microsoft—and I would've killed to work at Microsoft—but I had to turn them down because my commitment was the year off. And Facebook called me about running a piece of their business in China, and even though I was sure they'd never talk to me again, I gritted my teeth and said no. I had to know if the dream was real. I had to see it through for all twelve months.

In the last four months of that year away from work, I worked on my Clearing the Bar stories. What are those? Well, you know how some people will sit around the bar and talk about their dreams and goals, but never actually follow through? They'll sprinkle in a lot of "if onlys," like "If I could only get the money together, I'd buy a boat," or "If I could only get the time off work, I'd backpack across Asia."

Sometimes those dreams and goals are idle fantasizing, and the people telling those stories just want to kick around wild ideas with their buddies. But that's not how I'm wired. If I sit around the bar and share a dream aloud, it's because I really want to make it happen. I'd spent a lot of years in a lot of bars floating my stories, and I wanted to knock some of those things off my list. I wanted to clear the bar of those stories and turn some "if onlys" into realities.

To start, I reconnected with Ben. Remember Ben? My college friend who ended up bankrupt because of how we first invested in Austin? Well, back in those days, when we were working on the houses we co-owned, we'd talk about going to Graceland together. So my first order of business during my Clearing the Bar months was to get his ass to the Jungle Room (Elvis's man cave). I drove up to his home, rang his doorbell, and said, "Today's the day we go to Graceland." And we did. And it was wonderful.

Then I bought my mom a house, so she never had to worry about paying bills again for the rest of her life. One of my cousins was from a tiny town and always talked about traveling, even though he couldn't afford to go anywhere. When he graduated from high school, I took him to Belize to go diving. I helped a relative pay off some oppressive debts. It felt amazing to use my wealth to support the people I loved.

As the year started drawing to a close, I knew I'd need a compelling reason to go back to work again in technology. So I created one: I went out and bought myself a shiny new shopping center and an apartment complex. And I said, "That's my reason to go back to work. I can't take any money out of these new investments, and I'm up to my ass in debt. Time to head back to the office."

I went back to work, and I worked for an absolutely amazing four years.

Then I did it all again. Another year off, another twelve months of art, travel, and education. Since then I've been to Tahiti and Australia and Russia. I've climbed Everest and Kilimanjaro. I've visited Angkor Wat in Cambodia and been on safari and seen the *Mona Lisa*. And that cycle—four years at work, one year off—has been my template for life ever since.

How Will *You* Spend It?

You can only spend two things, money and time. I know that's been said a million times, but it's so true. I use my years off work to reconnect with old friends, to learn new things, to see the world, to challenge myself. And running my life this way makes me happy.

And that's the point. Rich isn't the point. If you ask me, even financial independence isn't really the point. The point is to find a way to live your life that makes you feel happy and fulfilled, challenged and alive. In most cases you need an abundance of time and money to make those feelings possible. That's a hard truth, but a real one. I could never have gone on any of my own adventures without plenty of time and money, and I continue to earn so I can continue to go on adventures. (To date, I have been to sixty-six countries.)

Neither money nor time will be infinite for any of us. So it comes down to priorities. It comes down to setting situations up so you can do the things that feel important and satisfying and real. Poet Mary Oliver wrote, "Tell me, what is it you plan to do with your one wild and precious life?"

Whatever it is, here's my advice to you:

1. Set specific and measurable goals.
2. Get started now.
3. Don't overthink it.

And once you've got the rough costs and drawbacks sketched out, once you've set a timeline, once you know for sure what you want to chase, ask yourself: "Am I committed to doing this? Am I willing to do what it takes, step-by-step, over multiple years, to make this a reality? Can I course correct along the way, with help from mentors and guides? Will this make me happy?"

CHAPTER 3

Keep Your Day Job. And Get a Second One.

IF YOU'RE SCRATCHING YOUR HEAD at this chapter title, allow me to explain.

Yes, I set a goal of earning $10,000 a month without working. And yes, I crushed that goal. But you may have noticed that I had a lot of jobs along the way. I worked at the barbecue restaurant, I tended bar, I helped Tom fix up his rental houses, I bought and ran my own rental houses, and eventually I got a string of sweet office jobs in tech. Am I a liar or a hypocrite? Nope.

That $10K rolls in every month whether I'm pulling a paycheck or not. I just know from experience that pulling a paycheck makes saving and investing my money a hell of a lot easier. In fact, I think anyone who wants to have an impressive chunk of change in the bank should be working not just one job but two. And here's why I cling to this wildly unpopular opinion.

Financially Independent People Are Not Average

If you're going to get ahead of the averages, you need to do something beyond average. If you want to have $1 million in the bank before age thirty-five, you can't just get a desk job and save your pennies like crazy. You need to be more radical than that. You need to push harder if you want to get ahead of the pack.

Start by looking up some labor statistics. Find out how much someone makes per year in the job you have or aspire to, on average, if they're your age and live in your town. Now consider that 21 percent of American workers don't save *anything*, and another 20 percent save 5 percent or less of their annual income.[1] That means that the vast majority of Americans will fall short of their savings needs when retirement time rolls around. But it also means that being above average in the savings game doesn't mean setting aside half your paycheck; it means saving more than 5 percent of your earnings. (It also means investing. But hang with me, we'll get there.)

Not too scary, right? And probably something you knew in your gut. Act average and you'll stay average. If you want to be an A student, or even a B student, you're going to have to study a little more than the C students. If you save the same amount everyone else saves, you're going to end up where they do.

Now, here's the scary part.

By age sixty-five, one-third of average Americans are dead.[2] And when they die, they have no net worth. In fact, most of them are $60,000 in debt.[3] They've spent an entire lifetime working but have accumulated nothing of value in case they keep living. They're dead broke, or just dead.

And those people are not bad people, or stupid people. They tried. They worked. They led perfectly normal lives. They just weren't able to push themselves beyond the averages.

But you, my friend, are well on your way to leaving the averages far behind you. You bought this book! And you got past the first three sentences of a chapter commanding you to work two jobs. Just by seeking financial education, you're giving yourself an advantage.

However, it's going to take more than knowledge and savvy to reach financial independence. It's going to take hard work. And lots of it. At two different day jobs.

Why I Went Corporate

Let's rewind to when Ben and I bought all those houses, put an assload of money on his credit cards, and he went bankrupt. The court left me with a handful of properties in my name, which meant I needed to find ways to pay them down and eventually pay them off.

So every single dollar I made at the barbecue restaurant was going into paying these debts down. But there was no money left over for me to live on.

So I got in touch with my mentor Tom, and asked for his advice. We looked at the contracts and made simple amortization tables available through a standard search, and he helped me set a goal—a date by which I'd have 30 percent equity in these properties. Because once I had that, I could refinance.

This was a strategy Tom used on his own properties. Once he'd paid a property down and had 30 percent equity in that property, he would refinance the principal only. Say he had a $100,000 house, for which his mortgage payment was $1,000 per month. When you've built up 30 percent equity on a $100,000 home, that's the equivalent of $30,000, you still owe $70,000 on it, but if you refinance after thirty-six months of payments, your new monthly mortgage payment is $700. Which creates $300 in profit per month, which used to go toward the mortgage, but now it comes directly to you. (This is an example that I created out of thin air. In the real world, interest rates fluctuate constantly, banks offer a wide variety of terms, and the math is a bit more involved. But I wanted to give you a simplified look at the benefits of refinancing to show how you can make more faster in the long run.)

How do you build equity quickly? You make extra payments. You outrun the interest so more of your money is going toward paying off the principal. (I'll come back to building equity later with more helpful tips.)

Which is why my mentor told me to give up my hippie-ass lifestyle (at least for now) and get a big-boy job. Otherwise, paying off these properties would take too damned long. Sure, I'd get there someday, but I'd be fifty by the time I did it.

That was not the plan. The plan was $10K a month without working by age thirty-six. So I ended up asking myself, "What kind of job can I get that'll make me enough to pay down these houses fast?"

Obviously, bartending wasn't going to cut it. And that's when I went into technology.

I got my first tech job in sales to get myself in a better financial position with all of my rental properties. Simple as that. I needed to make more money—ideally a lot more money—so I could deal with my debts like a grown-up. An interesting and unexpected thing started to happen: I realized that the corporate world could give me more than steady paychecks. It could give me financial and operational knowledge, a network, and insight into how people a hell of a lot smarter than I am dealt with problems a hell of a lot larger than those I faced in my little business.

Make Your Day Job a Paid Education

There are definite downsides to day jobs, especially corporate ones. They are full of other people's rules and other people's deadlines, and many of us hate feeling like we've got to color inside the lines. I served in the Air Force as a way of getting my college paid for, and I did fine in the military, but I didn't love it. All the rules, the uniforms, the sameness, the chain of command, it all chafed. And before I landed my tech job, I assumed that corporate work would feel similarly stifling. Nothing but seemingly arbitrary rules, and people who are forced to follow them.

But once I got inside this company, an interesting thing happened. I found I was meeting people I never would've met otherwise. People with finance degrees, people with marketing degrees, people who were wizards at sales and operations. These folks had all the skills that I would need to learn if I wanted to be an entrepreneur. And these folks were all right there in front of me, some of them underutilized and bored out of their skulls. So I decided to see them as a free teaching service.

As I've said, I failed college math three times, and to this day I have a recurring nightmare where I don't finish college math and can't graduate. (Anyone ever studied why the entire school-going world has school-related nightmares forever? Just saying.) Much later in life, I was diagnosed with mild dyslexia, and when that happened, I finally understood why I'll always need to quadruple-check my numbers. When I got that first day job, I just had a terrible track record and a massive fear of math.

But I went into sales anyway, which meant I had to learn how to calculate quotas. I needed to know how I got paid because I was there to maximize my paycheck. I took that sales job so I could make extra payments on my rental properties. I was forced to face my fears and get comfy with math.

I would sit down with my manager and say, "Hey, I've got to make an extra $200 or $300 this next paycheck. What can I sell? How can I sell it? Who's selling it better than me?"

Because I'm totally that guy. Chatty and ballsy and unafraid to ask for help from virtual strangers. And boy, did it pay off.

By the third week selling, I was the top salesperson in my training class. And when people would ask, "What did you do differently?" I would say, "I had to learn how to calculate my own paycheck, my own quotas. So I asked the best salespeople in the company to help me."

Are you picking up on one of Brady's Major Themes? It's mentoring, friend. Ongoing mentorships are amazing, but single-serve ones can be just as useful. Anytime you ask someone who's more of an expert than you are for their advice and guidance, you're getting mentored. And that is gold.

Anyway, I would look for the top sellers of a specific product and ask, "How did you learn to sell that product so well?" And they would sit down and tell me. Seriously. Nobody ever pushed back. Nobody ever said, "Hell no, kid, I'm not gonna share my secrets." They were all happy to help.

And I'll tell you why. Because at an international company, people are not competing against each other; they're competing against the outside competition. Most global companies split up sales territories either by state or by division, not by product or specialty. You're never really competing internally, which means sharing knowledge and resources is no big deal. So the whole "paid education" thing might be harder to hack at a smaller company, depending on your role as an employee, but at multinational companies? It is usually encouraged.

As I pursued my own paid education, I didn't just hit up the other salespeople. Since I had to sell into a territory, I knew I needed a marketing plan. So I would find someone in marketing to help me with that. That marketing knowledge spilled over into my work as a budding real estate mogul, since renting houses took marketing know-how, too. And then? I realized operations knowledge was what I needed as much as financial skills. Operations is basically a whole department of people who are paid to make the business more efficient. Lunching with those folks showed me how to manage my properties more cost effectively. For instance, one of them suggested I paint all of the houses the same color—at least on the inside—so I could buy the paint in bulk, which would be a lot cheaper. My operations buddies had me buying light bulbs and cleaning supplies in bulk, too, saving me money I didn't even know I could save.

I started scheduling biweekly one-on-one discussions with folks from finance who would sit down and explain to me exactly how my paycheck was calculated and how to get more out of it. But they did so much more. Most finance people are entrepreneurs at heart, which is why they were bursting with advice on my real estate investments. I'd show my little company's balance sheet to an actual finance MBA, and they'd geek out about it.

"Holy crap. Did you think about paying it off this way, Brady?"

Well, no, I didn't.

"What if you could only get a quarter point off your interest rate? What would that do for you?"

Well, I wasn't thinking about that.

"Oh yeah, here's how you calculate that."

Because that's what they do in their spare time, right? That's their zone of genius. They've got all this knowledge to share, so when someone comes along and says, "Share it with me," they're all over it.

And even beyond the specialized departmental knowledge, I learned about big business tactics. I got to observe what a multinational company does in crisis and learn from their wins and losses. I saw that leadership had strategies to take the company through bad times as well as good ones, and that they had rubrics to tell them when things were bad enough to require action. I watched how managers and executives worked to minimize surprises and anticipate trends in the market.

Working at a multinational company—or even a well-run national or local one—gives you more than just medical coverage. It can be an education, if you let it. And, in my opinion, you should. Because just like big businesses, entrepreneurs need sales, marketing, finance, and operations help. And building relationships with your colleagues at a global firm is a smart way to recruit that help while you're still pulling that steady paycheck.

The Value of a Second Job

You're on board with the idea of a day job, maybe even a corporate one. But you're still wondering about this whole "two jobs at once" thing that I sprang on you a few pages ago. Well, kids, lemme tell you a story.

When my parents got divorced, I was three years old. My dad never paid child support, so it was just my mom and me, and she made a conscious effort to treat us like a two-person team. It was like she was telling me, "We're going to have to do this on our own." I could feel that. And I got on board.

Money was tight, and my mom asked if we could move back in with her parents, my grandparents. The deal they struck was that we could live with them only if she would go back to college. She had quit school thinking that she was going to get married and live the dream. Her husband was going to take care of her. But that fell apart.

I'm not sure if it was her attempt to ground me in reality or make me a self-sufficient boy—someone who wouldn't pin his dreams to another person—but my mom was always straight with me. She'd say things like, "I have to go to school today. You're going to stay here with Grandma and Grandpa, but I have to go to school so I can get a job so we can live by ourselves." Plain language, conveying ideas that made me aware of money at a young age.

She studied elementary education, became a schoolteacher, and made it clear that her salary was small. But the trade-off was that her job allowed her to spend lots of time with me. We had enough to get our own place, but not enough for much else.

When I was in fourth grade, my mom asked me, "Do you want to go to Disneyland this summer? We have cousins who live in California, and I was thinking we could stay with them."

Well, of course I wanted to go to Disneyland. Is there any place cooler when you're a kid?

But then she was really honest with me and she said, "If we're going to go to Disneyland, I've got to make enough money so we can afford it. I don't have enough money now, but here's how I could afford it by summertime. I could get another job."

And we sat down at the kitchen table to look at her notes. She had a rough idea of how much it was going to cost for the two of us to go to Disneyland, and she'd worked up a budget for gas and lodging along the way.

"We'll have to drive there, and we will eat sandwiches along the way," she said. "We won't be stopping for dinner anywhere. We're going to stop at a grocery store to get supplies to make our own food, which will be much cheaper. And then when we get there, we'll go sleep at our cousins' house. So it won't be easy, and we'll have to cut some corners, but if we do this right, we can make it work."

"That's all fine," I said. "But you said you have to get another job. What does that mean?"

She said, "If we're going to do this, we'll have to do this together, and I'm going to get a second job as a cashier at a grocery store. I'll work there at night. And I'll save all the money from that job so that we can go to Disneyland together."

I nodded.

"That means I won't be home when you get back from school," she explained. "You're going to be home by yourself for five hours. Can you do that? Are you willing to do that until summer?"

I was. So we did it.

Now, my mom wasn't gone every night, but she was gone a couple of nights every week at first. Once I got used to being on my own and could make sandwiches for my dinner, she worked her way up to four nights a week. And she would come home and, God love her, check my home-work and talk to me until I went to sleep so that I knew that everything was okay.

And every night as she was tucking me in, she would say, "I made twenty dollars tonight, to go into the Disneyland fund. So now we only have to make another thousand."

And at first I would groan or make a face, because, my God, that sounded insurmountable.

And she would say, "No, no, no! Every day I'm going to make another twenty dollars, which means I don't have to do this forever. I just have to do it one step at a time. We're twenty dollars closer to Disneyland, and that's good."

And sure enough, that summer we went to Disneyland.

Two years later, we went to Disney World, and two years after that, we drove all the way to Yellowstone. I'd come back from summer vacation feeling like a world explorer. Somewhere in there I started understanding that I could do big things, but I might have to be a grocery store cashier *and* a schoolteacher to do them.

A second income gives you flexibility and power. A second job gives you an entire discrete income to apply to your goals and dreams. A second job allows you to learn more about yourself and the world. Yeah, you'll be tired. Yeah, you won't want to do it forever. But this is one of the key ways to set yourself apart from the averages. Get a second job, bring in a second income, and you're instantly positioned to save and invest more.

Quick caveat: I'm assuming, here, that you have just one job and have both the ability and the bandwidth to add a second. If you're already juggling three part-time gigs and need every penny of your earnings to keep yourself (and possibly others) afloat, this advice won't work for you. You're already maxed out on job-working. So feel free to skim or skip and find other nuggets of investment wisdom that work with your life and situation.

Why Everyone Should Consider Working Two Jobs

Think you should just live frugally and save more of your current pay-check? Think you'd be better off finding a super-high-paying day job? Think you'd rather just play the lotto?

By all means, try those things. Truth is, this is just one way to reach financial independence. But it's a really good way. Here's why.

On top of giving you a stream of income that you can use solely to build your savings or your investment portfolio, taking a second job allows you to try out these options:

Do something different: Do you work in telemarketing all day? Take a second job as a pet sitter! Do you supervise a biomedical lab? Take a second job painting houses! Many of us get so stuck in the idea of building a single-track career, we forget about other ways to earn money doing jobs that are wildly different from our primary ones and that utilize different parts of our brains. If you think all day, take a second job doing something physical, or vice versa.

Fill in the holes in your education: Did you learn how to change a tire at school? How to landscape a yard? How to perform CPR? Even PhDs have gaps. Taking a second job is a fantastic way to learn while working. If you aren't interested in skills or physical tasks, think about tutoring. Or working as a research assistant. This is an opportunity to become a well-rounded adult.

Have fun while earning: Maybe you adore your primary day job. If you do, that's awesome; working stiffs everywhere are jealous of you. But if your primary day job suits your skill set and pays well but doesn't exactly thrill you, taking a second job can help you remember that some work is fun. Bartending is guaranteed to connect you with interesting folks and give you hilarious stories to tell. Working with animals or plants is rewarding in ways that office work will never be. Caring for seniors and kids can be challenging, but also hilarious and enriching. Make your second job the fun one.

Build yourself up as an expert: If you're already pretty far along in your primary career journey, a second job could help you become even fancier and more impressive. Take a board position with a salary. Consult with companies in your field. Create a side gig that augments your main gig and pads out your resume with impressive accomplishments.

Address your weaknesses: Maybe you're like me and have always struggled with math. A job in retail will force you to hone your arithmetic skills. Maybe you're naturally soft-spoken and wish you were a better communicator. Sales of any kind will force you to polish up your people skills. Maybe you're intimidated by computers. Working at an electronics store will give you an education by immersion. Your second job can be leveraged for personal or professional development in the best possible ways.

Your primary job will cover your living expenses. Your second job will feed your investments. I strongly recommend working them both until your investments reach critical mass. Once you can pay for all of your living expenses with the income from your investments, you can drop down to one job. Maybe even a part-time job. But until then, two jobs will get you to your goals much faster than just one.

But I've Got Kids

Yeah. Kids. They do complicate things.

If you're in family-building mode and taking on a second job feels like a real stretch, this might not be the solution for you. That's legit. Spending time with your kids (and partner, if you're lucky enough to have one of those) is extremely important. I've got two kids myself, and they are the absolute light of my life, so I have no desire to tear you away from yours.

But here's a quick reminder that my own mom worked two jobs to achieve her financial goals, and seeing her do that had a huge positive impact on me. It wasn't easy for either of us, but it was possible. Even beneficial.

If you want to hold down two jobs, and you've got growing kids, there are workarounds. If they're school-aged, you can wake up two hours earlier or go to sleep two hours later than normal and use that time to freelance from home. You can enlist your extended family to help with childcare, which has the added bonus of allowing your kids to foster close relationships with their other relatives. If you have a partner, you can work out a schedule that puts them in charge when you're working; only one of you needs a second job, so lean on your other half for added support. Depending on what kind of second job you take, you can even bring your kids with you. Teach them about work and dedication, goals and finances by exposing them to those things directly.

If you're just cringing at the thought of being away from your kiddos, then find another way. But promise me you'll find it. Your kids will thrive if you are financially independent. Your kids shouldn't keep you from doing something that will benefit the whole family.

Other Perks of Corporate Work

Let's circle back to the whole corporate job thing for a moment. I definitely believe that one of your jobs can be something nontraditional, weird, and fun that fills a need in your life. But I also believe that taking a job with an established national or multinational company is a smart move. Yeah, start-ups are sexy, but they have a terrible habit of imploding. And mom-and-pops have heart, but often lack the resources that larger organizations inevitably have. So, if the very idea of working at a traditional corporation makes you itchy and irate, I'm gonna have to take you by the ear, sit you down, and give you a talking-to.

We already discussed how corporate jobs can be educational and how you can mine your coworkers for knowledge and advice, even while you're on the clock. And I pointed out that all entrepreneurs and career investors benefit from having sales, marketing, finance, and operations know-how. But here's what else you get when you take a job at a legacy company with deep pockets and a robust HR department:

Free or subsidized education: If you can make a case—even a ridiculously flimsy case—that a degree or class will help you do your job better, I guarantee your employer will find a way to pay for it. Multinational companies love to cover college and vocational tuition for their employees, since it makes them look like they care (which they often do) and since it builds loyalty and morale.

Commissions and bonuses: Want some extra money on top of your regular money? Work in a sales department with a commission structure, or a large company that offers annual or performance-based bonuses. These types of pay bumps are far easier to come by in large, stable corporations.

Retirement support: Pensions may be a thing of the past, but the vast majority of global corporations offer retirement programs such as 401(k)s and 403(b)s. The best among them will encourage you to set aside as much as possible by matching a percentage of your monthly investment. Saving for retirement as an individual or a self-employed person is unbelievably hard. In fact, saving for retirement as *any* person is hard. (Proof: 49 million Americans have $0 set aside for retirement.[4]) Why not get help from your employer?

Stock options and profit sharing: Some large corporations, including Walmart and Apple, offer employee-purchased stock options to their workforce. They allow employees to purchase stock at a reduced price once or twice a year, and employees who participate in the program can put a percentage of each paycheck toward those stock purchases. Others offer profit-sharing plans in which employees receive a percentage of a company's profits based on its quarterly or annual earnings. Nonprofits and small businesses can't offer similar perks. This stuff is specific to the big boys.

Medical, dental, vision: Yes, smaller companies often offer these. But bigger ones get better deals from the healthcare providers and pass that savings on to their employees. Paying for your own insurance is a huge financial burden. When you work for a large corporation, your costs are typically lower because you're splitting them with an employer who can purchase policies at a discount.

Reliable paycheck: Obvious? Yup. Still worth mentioning? Double yup. The security of knowing that you'll be getting a certain amount of money every couple of weeks, come hell or high water, is a huge relief.

A less obvious perk: Holding a traditional, professional job with a giant multinational corporation makes you a better candidate for loans. Banks will love you. And if you're going to become a serial investor, you will need banks to love you.

So there's my little love song to corporate America. Short, sweet, and hopefully convincing. But it does have one big, fat caveat.

Work for a Plan, Not a Promotion or a Title

If you decide to take my advice and get a cushy-sounding corporate job, promise me you won't get so snowed by internal politics that you'll start gunning for a fancy title. Because the point of a cushy corporate job is money. Financial security. Benefits and stability. Does being the Senior VP of Widgets get you any of those things? Maybe and maybe not. The point is to not get so focused on a title that you lose focus on the main thing—your own financial independence.

I had this point driven home for me a few years ago when I hired a woman out of New York to be my corporate coach. (Mentorship! You can and should pay for it.) I was trying to land my next big job at the next Fortune 500 company and wanted her to help me strategize.

She said to me, "Now this job that you're getting. Are you more interested in the title and the promotion, or are you more interested in the money?"

And I said, "Are you kidding me?"

"Nope," she said. "It's a solid game in the world. Lots of companies are more than happy to give you a title because they know some people love to walk around and tell everyone they're the brand-new President of Whatever. They love having a fabulous business card with a fabulous title on it. So, is that you? Or are you after the money? Which one's more important to you?"

I said, "Well, the money, for God's sake. The only reason I'm doing this is for money, but I would like to have both if possible."

"Okay, so even if we found you a job making more money, you would prioritize money over title?" she asked. "Hopefully we can get you both, but if we can get you just the money, is that more important than a title?"

Again, I was flabbergasted.

"Yeah. Just the money would be great."

"Good," she said. "I'm with you on that. When I'm in line at the grocery store, I always ask myself, 'Would they take someone's job title in lieu of cash?' And I always know the answer."

What's that you're saying? Impressive titles often come with big pay raises? Well, sometimes they do and sometimes they don't. In fact, sometimes impressive titles come with increased responsibility but flat pay. Companies know that people see title changes as markers of success, and that sometimes we'll accept more work for the same payout if we get to call ourselves something fancy.

And it's BS. Don't fall for it. Work for the money, and work so you can move toward financial independence. Do *not* work for a title.

And while you're at it, do not work for a promotion. I have a great friend who spent an entire year prepping because his boss, a VP, had a "plan." This friend skipped out on a vacation so he could prep for the next year's promotion. And, of course, the company "changed directions." His boss's promise vanished into thin air, and he found out he'd wasted a metric ton of time and effort. Point being, you may choose to go after a juicy promotion, but the corporation never owes you anything. Nothing is guaranteed, so don't work yourself to death over the possibility of moving up.

Corporate jobs, steady jobs with established companies, and high-paying jobs with stability can be essential parts of your plan for financial independence. In fact, I think they should be part of your plan. The trick is to do the work, do your best, and be successful without buying into the corporate culture of manufactured importance. Be wary of society's rubber-stamped markers of success, things like titles and promotions and bogus awards. Don't let 'em snow you. Stick to your plan. Take the perks, take the paycheck, but never let anyone convince you that a fair reward for hard work is a new business card with a fancy new title on it. I hope you get the benefits of both.

Work More Now to Work Less Later

I get it. Working multiple jobs doesn't sound glamorous or fun. And it won't be all of the time. Take it from someone who did it for decades. But working two jobs is a foolproof way to earn more and learn more as you learn the ropes of investing. (Which we'll be digging into in the coming chapters.) And if you work more now—ideally toward the beginning of your career—you'll be able to work less later. Work to invest, invest wisely, and then taper off the working, and you'll be sitting pretty well before retirement.

Even if you've never met with a financial planner, you've probably heard some money guru sing the praises of diversification, which is just a fancy word for making money in several different ways at once. And it's a simple but important investment practice that everyone—and I mean everyone—should use. It's the money equivalent of "don't put all your eggs in one basket." Successful entrepreneurs don't turn up their noses at hard work or smart investing. They know that both have their place on the road to success. And most of the richest people in the world make money in multiple ways simultaneously. So should you.

Now, go out and get yourself a second job. I'll wait right here.

CHAPTER
4

The Three Incomes: Earned, Investment, and Passive

INVESTMENT INCOME IS EASY ENOUGH to understand. It is money made from investments. But some income is made from selling something, like a stock. This is a standard transfer of sale, and if you sell for more than you paid, then congratulations.

The kind of money I wanted was an income stream from my investments. This is steady, predictable income, such as rental income. This income, too, is investment income. I envisioned a portfolio of properties and stocks that were sending me $10,000 per month even if I was in Bora Bora. I wanted it to be as automatic as possible. But $10,000 a month was a big hill to climb. Luckily, an accountant friend told me that it might be a little easier than I thought because investment income is taxed at a lower rate than earned or salaried income.

So there is a double benefit to increasing the amount of investment dollars we have at work. One, it can be predictable for long periods of time, like rental income and dividend paying stocks. A secondary benefit is that investment income is taxed at nearly half of the top tax bracket.

At the time of this writing, the top income bracket is taxed at 37 percent while investment income or capital gains tax is 20 percent. Yes, the system rewards people who invest with a 17 percent tax benefit versus earned income. This can make a very big difference in the amount of money you see in your pocket. Let's say you make $500,000 at your salaried and commissioned job. Congrats on the six-figure club! How much will you pay in taxes at the top rate? $500,000 × .37 = $185,000. Your take-home pay will be $315,000.

Now let's compare that to passive and investment income taxed at 20 percent. Same salary, $500,000 × .20 = $100,000 in taxes—a difference in take-home pay of $85,000.

As always, I am going to refer you to an accountant for changes or corrections based on your particular situation. But the point is the same: we want more investment income over time than earned income.

A Crash Course in Passive Income

As I've mentioned, passive income is simply money being earned regularly with little or no effort on the part of the person earning it. When you get down to brass tacks, there are three basic ways to make this type of income:

1. Investing in stocks, bonds, and markets
2. Creating or investing in a business
3. Investing in real estate

These three have been around for ages and are unlikely to disappear anytime soon. Most ridiculously wealthy people dabble in all three, but make most of their money through just one of these avenues. If you're serious about becoming a skillful investor, you're going to spend a ton of time researching, interviewing, thinking, crunching numbers, consulting experts, and making tough decisions. This will become a hobby on steroids before it becomes a true profession. So if you focus on something you hate, you'll be miserable. Don't do that. Whichever of these three investment income streams intrigues you most is the one you should pursue.

For me, that was real estate. (Surprised? Then you've clearly skipped chapters one to three.) But if *you* find the notion of buying and renting properties to be mind-numbingly dull, listen to your gut!

Furthermore, do not buy into the notion that any of these passive income streams are "too hard" or "only for rich folks." Do you need to have money to invest? Yes. Does that money have to be all yours? Nope. And do you need to have a shit-ton of it before you can get going? Also no. Passive income is a long game, which means you can start small and increase your spending incrementally or not at all. Think like a start-up: You can have $2,000, then throw in with four buddies who also have $2,000, and sink your collective $10,000 into a start-up company. You can buy a single share of Apple stock today and make a goal of buying another share each month for the next five years. You can buy your first property with no money down like I did. And once you start getting returns on your small investments, you can funnel it back into slightly larger ones. And on and on until you can join the ranks of the wealthy who pay dinky amounts of taxes and bring in boatloads of capital gains. And when that happens, I expect a thank-you note.

But even if you never get to that point, I hope you'll start to dabble in passive income streams. They are incredibly beneficial to absolutely all living, breathing human beings because they do this for you:

- Protect you from a complete loss of income if you're fired or furloughed from your day job
- Help you accumulate wealth slowly but surely
- Make it easier to retire early
- Provide an additional source of income when you're no longer able to work
- Make you a more financially informed and savvy person

The income we make from hourly or salaried jobs doesn't stick around. Passive income streams, on the other hand, pave a path to sustainable wealth.

Know who taught me that? My granddaddy.

"And Up from the Ground Came a Bubblin' Crude. (Oil, That Is. Black Gold. Texas Tea.)"

Now, you've met my granddaddy before, but let me tell you a little more about him. He only had a third-grade education. He started three businesses that all failed, but the fourth one worked. He died with a net worth of nearly a million dollars sometime in the mid-1990s.

For me, the greatest part about spending time with my grandfather was listening to him and learning from him. Somehow, he was able to take what he'd learned, distill it all, and relay it to me in interesting and memorable ways. That man was a master storyteller.

He loved to trot out the parable of the king and the architect, which I now trot out for my own kids and will trot out for you right now.

My granddaddy would start, "Say I offer you a job, Brady. You can either get paid a penny a day, but that amount would double each day you work, or you could just get paid $100 a day. Which is the better deal?"

Well, every kid you've ever met snaps up that $100-a-day rate! Including me. So my granddaddy followed up with this story.

Once there was a king who wanted to build a palace, so he called in the royal architect and together they drew up the most beautiful palace the world had ever seen. The king asked the architect, "How much will this cost to build?"

And the architect said, "Tell you what. Rather than worrying about the total cost, you can pay me one penny today, two pennies tomorrow, four pennies on the third day, and just keep doubling it every day until the building is done."

And the king, who was no dummy, could see he'd be getting a great deal.

He said, "Sure, I'll do that."

So the architect took out a chessboard to keep track of their accounting. On the first day, he came to work and the king put a penny on the chessboard; on the second day he put down two; on the third day he put four down and thought to himself, "Man, I'm getting the greatest deal!"

But by the ninth day, the king was laying down 256 pennies. By the twelfth day he owed $20.48. By the end of the month, the king was paying $5,368,709.12 for *just one day of work*. And by the time the two men had filled up that chessboard, guess what had happened? The architect owned the entire kingdom. The king was out of money.

Why am I making you listen to a kids' story? Because we forget facts, but remember stories. And this story shows us that it's better to be patient and understand math than it is to go for the quick money. Investing is a long game. Get in early, don't be afraid to start small, and cultivate patience.

My granddaddy practiced what he preached, and I got to see his investor's patience play out. His father was the smallest investor on four or five wells that are still pumping oil today, and my grandfather wisely followed up on that small family investment. After his third business tanked, he decided to sink some of the money he had left into those same wells.

He said, "I'm happy to be the smallest investor in these wells, and I don't plan on this being a huge moneymaker for me. I just want to get an extra $50 or $100 a month for the rest of my life."

"Really?" I said. "Will you start making that money right away?"

"I don't have to get paid up front," he explained. "I'll get paid over time. And then when I'm really old, this money will still be coming in. I won't want to work when I'm seventy, and if this investment pays out like I expect, I won't have to."

I was just a kid at the time, and talking about getting old bored me, so my eyes must've glazed over because my granddaddy cocked his head and looked at me.

"Listen, Brady. What I'm telling you is I'm working today for free, but I'm going to make $100 a month for the rest of my life off this well."

Now *that* I understood. That stuck with me.

And years later, when I was in my twenties and started researching passive income while working my barbecue jobs, I realized that artists' royalties were similar. A band puts in lots of hard work to produce a great recording and gets paid small amounts every time that recording is played on the radio, or in a movie, or over a commercial. As I interviewed more and more rich folks during that time period, I saw that real estate could also fit the work-now-get-paid-forever paradigm. And since I wasn't destined to be a rock star or an oil tycoon, I started buying up houses like a madman. (As you know because you've read chapter one.)

Now, listen. If you feel like you're not destined to be a rock star or an oil tycoon, and you couldn't give a flying rat's ass about the stock market, there are other options. Those three tried-and-true avenues for passive income are the safest bets, but some others have emerged over the years. One of them is bound to suit you.

Lesser-Known Passive Income Streams

Let's start with mineral rights, which my granddaddy bought to make his money. When you think of minerals, you might think about zinc and calcium and other stuff that you can buy in the health food aisle, and you're not wrong. But mineral rights also include everything from oil and natural gas to gold, copper, and diamonds.

What does that mean? Well, usually when you buy a piece of real estate, you get the rights to the building and the "ground" it sits on. You can also purchase the rights to what sits below the building and ground, whatever that may contain, or "air rights" to the space above a property. When you buy mineral rights, you're buying the right to exploit, mine, or produce any minerals lying below the surface of the property.

Most of us don't own mineral rights to the properties we own. Most of us don't live in areas rich in oil and natural gas, and most of us don't own drilling equipment, so we don't even think about purchasing mineral rights when we buy our homes. That's just fine. Because mineral rights are useless unless they are attached to a piece of land that actually yields something valuable, and it's smarter—especially when you're just getting started—to sink money into a sure thing.

Big oil and gas companies like Exxon, Shell, and Chevron are experts at finding great properties and have entire departments of people dedicated to buying up mineral rights. So if you buy shares in your favorite oil and gas syndicate, you are essentially investing in mineral rights.

If you want something less corporate, you can investigate properties on your own. Some owners will sell mineral rights on their own properties, which you can buy outright or partially. You can also buy either a working interest (which involves installing a new well, or drilling/digging from scratch) or an operating interest (which involves buying shares in an existing well or a drilling/digging operation). As you can imagine, operating interests are far easier for newbie investors to manage.

Side note: You don't pay taxes on mineral rights until someone drills and is successful. You'll need to put money toward the investment itself, but no taxes are owed until the property starts barfing up oil or natural gas or buckets of gold nuggets. Sweet deal, right?

Unless you get really into the whole mining scene and start setting up your own drills all over creation, mineral rights are among the most passive of the passive income streams. You give someone money, wait, and get paid whenever they hit pay dirt. If you're interested in something more creative and active, you've got other options.

Songwriters and book authors have used the royalties system of payment since the Dark Ages. They do the creative heavy lifting at the front end, get help from a publisher or distributor to make sure the work reaches the masses, and get paid tiny amounts over time. (For songs, it's payment for plays. For books, it's payment for copies sold.) But today? Creative types have many more opportunities.

What's your talent or skill? What can you do or teach that others value? Even if you can't write a song or a book about it, can you record a video and share it on a YouTube channel or TikTok? Start an Instagram account documenting it? Teach a course online about it? Keep a blog that uses affiliate links to generate income? Selling your knowledge takes a lot more work than traditional investing, but it can be both rewarding and profitable.

Fashion blogger Blair Eadie, who runs Atlantic-Pacific, makes between $2,400 and $4,000 for a single Instagram post.[5] YouTuber Evan Fong posts videos about online gaming and made $11.5 million in 2019,[6] and makeup YouTuber Huda Kattan has leveraged her online fame into a business empire worth $550 million. Self-made coach and entrepreneur Danielle LaPorte charges about $30,000 for a speaking gig.[7] Of course, most creative folks hustled their hearts out for many years before raking in that kind of cash, and they trade their talents for money. So it's a little less passive than some of the other avenues we've explored in this chapter.

But smaller bloggers like Sarah Von Bargen of Yes and Yes or Melissa Ingold of TimeFreedomBusiness.com create and sell online courses for $17 to $297 a pop and bring in tens of thousands of dollars each year. Once the courses are written and filmed, the rest of the work is minimal: marketing, promoting, and collecting fees on content that's already been created.

If you love documenting your craft projects, meals, or pets, you can earn off an Instagram account: a middle-level influencer gets an average of $271 per Instagram post.[8] If you're an avid gamer, you can charge subscribers between $4.99 and $24.99 to subscribe to your streaming channel. And if none of these appeal to you, entrepreneur Pat Flynn's website Smart Passive Income has dozens of other ideas for generating ongoing income online.

If all else fails? Just call me. I've been helping people figure out how to invest and earn for decades, and I'd be happy to talk your ear off.

Stay Wealthy by *Not* Spending Your Money

The original title of this chapter was "How to Make Money Without Working," and now that I've written it, I realize that's the tiniest bit misleading. There's no real way to earn without working. There's always some work. There's always some exploration and investigation that needs to happen to set up your passive income streams. And if you decide to sell and market your expertise, your income may not be truly passive at all.

So I guess this chapter is really about ways to make money that don't involve sitting in a cubicle and pulling a flat salary. It's about strategies for working in a way that suits you, and for earning indefinitely over the long term.

But the real trick to financial independence isn't earning or investing. It's learning how *not* to spend the money you've accumulated. And that, my friends, is trickier for some of us than it is for others.

The folks who excel at both earning and saving money are nicknamed prodigious accumulators of wealth, or PAWs, by business professors Thomas Stanley and William Danko. When these two researchers set out to study the habits of the American millionaire, they wanted to see if the Hollywood paradigm of huge houses, sports cars, and conspicuous consumption would hold up. It didn't.

Stanley and Danko's classic book, *The Millionaire Next Door*, does a fantastic job of proving that American millionaires live well below their means, value financial independence over flash, and spend a staggering amount of their time studying their investment portfolios. These people drive Toyotas and wear Timex watches, they budget and control all of their expenses, and they set financial goals. These are not miserly Scrooge types swimming in gold coins, but they're also not spending like rock stars. They're smart men and women who are fascinated by all aspects of investment and who want to have enough savings in the bank to keep their families solvent for ten or more years.

And, like the wealthy people I chatted about at the beginning of the chapter, they work the system. These low-key millionaires build wealth by minimizing their earned income and maximizing their investment income so they can pay as little in income tax as possible. They've hit on that magic formula of earning, investing, and saving and do everything in their power to hold on to every penny they put in the bank.

In case you think these invisible millionaires are a myth, let's revisit my mentor Tom, the real estate mastermind who took me under his wing before I'd even bought a single house. Well, my initial introduction to Tom was actually in a college class. My sociology professor showed a video of a very normal-looking man being interviewed. He seemed to be some sort of construction worker and was likable and plainspoken. Maybe even shy. During the interview, he did not discuss his occupation or education.

Once the video was done, the professor asked us to fill out a questionnaire about our impressions of him. What did we think was his annual income? Did he have a college degree? Was he married? What kind of car did he drive? Like most of my classmates, I assumed he was a blue-collar worker who'd maybe done a bit of community college but didn't have much in the way of wealth.

Well, you've already heard the spoiler: Tom was actually a multimillionaire who owned more than a hundred rental houses and held a master's degree in electrical engineering. He just liked cutoff shorts and didn't want to work for anyone else. He saved the money he earned instead of spending it on expensive crap, and he had absolutely zero interest in hobnobbing with Austin's wealthy elite. My sociology prof did a bang-up job of proving that looks can be deceiving, and I earmarked Tom as someone I needed to meet.

The point of passive income is to build wealth. But if you set up five lines of passive income and spend every dime you earn, you're wasting your time and energy. Invest, earn, and save, my friends. Emphasis on the "save."

Invest Today So Tomorrow Will Be Easier

Why invest, earn, *and* save? Because my granddaddy told you to.

He pointed out the wisdom of working one day out of your life and getting paid forever and the vital importance of creating a financial safety net. You never know when lean times will hit, and you never want to be caught off guard. As the COVID-19 crisis of 2020–2021 proved, most Americans live paycheck to paycheck and are likely in trouble when those paychecks are disrupted (including many high earners!), as the Motley Fool observed in March 2020.[9] That's the opposite of financial independence. That's self-defeating dependence that can leave you destitute in a matter of months.

If you want to invest, earn, and save so you can live more comfortably, I say more power to you. Buy stuff. Travel. Set up your life how you'd like it to look. I hope, though, that you'll also do it as a way of planning for the future. Today is great, but tomorrow is coming in hot, and if you only get to enjoy your cushy life for a year or two, you'll be crabby as hell when it all evaporates. Invest a little now so you'll have a lot later. Invest slowly but surely to build that wealth. Pick your favorite flavor of passive income, bring in those capital gains, and sock it away.

CHAPTER
5

Compound Interest Is the Eighth
Wonder of the World

I HAVE HAD A FEAR of math for most of my life and had to overcome it to get
to this stage in my career. That said, I will try to make this exploration
of compound interest entertaining. If you, like me, have a fear of math,
know that you will have to work on overcoming it in order to invest.

To start, peek back at the parable of the king and the architect in
chapter four. That was a preview of your compound interest syllabus, an
introduction to the idea that patience and math are equally important
in the moneymaking game. In regular-guy terms, compound interest is
basically the snowball effect: as your investment grows, it gathers more
money, and the bigger it gets, the more interest it earns.

And the best news of all? Anyone with cash to invest can take advantage of this money multiplier.

Explain It to Me Like I'm Five Years Old

I used to be very confused and intimidated by financial terms. Many people are. A good example is the term *earned income*. Earned income, for the purposes of this book, refers to money you had to work for as opposed to money that your portfolio of investments worked for. Earned income includes salary plus bonuses or commissions, or an hourly wage times the number of hours you will work on average in a year.

An attorney friend of mine, when asking about someone's earned income, likes to ask, "How much did you report on your W-2 last year?" Now our accountant friends will want to make further distinctions here, but I would like to keep this discussion high level. If you want to take this up further, please call an accountant.

I have heard that Albert Einstein said, "Compound interest is the eighth wonder of the world." Whether he said this or not, I like to think it is true. The good news is that if you are planning on long-term investing, compound interest may be the best friend you have.

It surely has been in my case. Here is a real-life example of compounding interest.

In 1994, I was in college and bought a duplex for $28,000. I sold the duplex twenty-eight years later in 2022 for $269,000. That is a gross profit of $241,000.

That equates to roughly 8.75 percent appreciation per year (also called a Rate of Return).

That looks great on the surface, but remember you are comparing year one with year twenty-eight.

It was not a very cool story in year two, when it had appreciated only $2,450.

Here is the place most people lose interest and where investors get excited.

Why do people lose interest? Compounding takes time. It is not an immediate feedback loop. The average person will rightly look at the $2,450 the property appreciated in the first year and think it isn't much. For sure it is not the life-changing real estate story we see on TV.

On TV and even from books, we can get the initial impression that huge returns happen overnight. The truth is you want to build a healthy respect for the amount of time this could take. The great news is we can get a fairly accurate idea of how long it will take for a property to double in value, and that can give us a higher degree of confidence to wait until we get the profit we want.

In the first year, a $28,000 property with 8.75 percent interest appreciation has a $2,450 gain. Or, you can say the property is worth $30,450.

That does not look like much, but in the second year, the property starts at $30,450 and adds $2,664 for a total value of $33,114.

By the tenth year, the property, at the same appreciation rate of 8.75 percent, is now worth $59,569.

In the twentieth year, the value is $137,821, and so on.

What did I do to earn that $241,000 after twenty-eight years of ownership?

Answer: not much. I did the up-front work of identifying the property and then assembling a financial and management team to look after it for me, but after that, the property appreciated value without hands-on work from me.

And I kept collecting homes. Some years I bought one. Other years I bought three or four. But the main thing was that I got very acquainted with how compound interest worked on each investment property. Then it began to show something extraordinary.

And the properties kept compounding each year while I worked in tech. All I did was make sure I understood the financial reports and kept up with details through a management team. Sometimes I would go months without even seeing them. Yes, the management team was that good.

At some point in the fourth or fifth year, I began using the Rule of 72 to predict where my portfolio of properties was going. And then one of the greatest investing days ever happened.

I realized that using the Rule of 72 as a guideline for investing projection had led to equaling the six-figure salary I was making as a sales manager. Think about that. I had literally doubled my income and, best of all, I could predict that the next year I was likely to make more through investments than I would from my sales career.

And that was one of the greatest days of my life.

Even now I keep a spreadsheet and use a simple compound interest template to project where I will be five, ten, and twenty years from today.

You, too, can use the Rule of 72 to make projections about your financial future.

The Rule of 72 says that 72 divided by your compound interest rate equals the number of years before your investment doubles in value.

Rule of 72: 72 / compound interest rate = number of years for original investment to double in value

Example: 72 / 10 = 7.2

In this example, we used 10 as the interest rate or appreciation rate for the investment. At an interest rate of 10 percent, it will take an original investment amount 7.2 years to double in value.

So if you buy a property for $100,000, and the current average appreciation in the neighborhood equals 10 percent, how many years until the property is valued at $200,000? 7.2 years.

Even more fun than the Rule of 72 is the Rule of 114.

The Rule of 114 tells you the number of years before the investment triples. It has the same principle as the Rule of 72.

Example: 114 / 10 = 11.4

In this example, at an interest rate of 10 percent, the investment triples in value in 11.4 years.

So the property you purchased for $100,000 will be valued at $300,000 after 11.4 years.

Now here is the *real* question: What did you do to increase value other than buy the property and hold it? Like I did with my first property, very little.

This is as simple as it gets and an example of how the rich get richer. Imagine a property or group of investment worth $1,000,000.

Now let's say that property earns 10 percent in appreciation per year. How many years until our investment is worth $2,000,000?

72 / 10 = 7.2 years

Do you see what is happening here? A big number only gets bigger each year.

Why Normal Folks Should Care About Compound Interest

Reading through my journey, you can understand why I have a healthy dislike for credit card debt. Personally, I keep one, and no more than one, for travel bookings and emergencies. Let's just say that I learned that it's best if I don't keep the temptation around. Try it out.

Credit card debt also works on the Rule of 72, but in reverse. It tells you how long it will take for your *balance owed* to double. I want to type that sentence fifty more times to get the point across but have been advised that is not necessary.

Before I illustrate that point, let's start with a question. Pick the credit card you have in your wallet right now with the highest balance.

I will wait.

Now, off the top of your head, what is that card's balance and interest rate?

Don't know your card's interest rate?

Don't worry, no one else does either.

Write that down as homework.

Let's play the averages and see how fast a credit card balance can get out of hand.

At the time of this writing, the average credit card holder has roughly $5,000 in credit card debt.

The typical credit card has an average interest rate of 16 percent.

Using the Rule of 72, how long before that $5,000 equals $10,000?

72 / 16 = 4.5 years

These numbers are simplified for the demonstration, but you get the point. The Rule of 72 can work against you, so make sure you know what you are paying and have a plan for it.

The point is that you do not need to be a math whiz in order to make investing work for you. Even better, you can evaluate your own investments and debts and project what they'll look like in the near and distant future. Are they working for you or against you? And, just as important, at what rate are they accelerating?

Slow Investing = Eating Your Vegetables

Compound interest is downright miraculous stuff, but it ain't speedy. As you work your way through this dazzling and highly entertaining chapter, you'll notice that all of the investment avenues it covers require a buttload of time and patience. If giving a buddy $5,000 for his tech start-up is like taking a shot of tequila, buying into a REIT is eating a big ol' plate of broccoli. Slow investing isn't sexy, but it works.

Here's the proof.

I joined the military to pay for college. I joined the US Air Force because I knew my mom didn't have the money to send me, because I wasn't 100 percent ready for college after high school wrapped up, and because I was itching to see more of the world.

I became a medic, which meant I worked in a hospital surrounded by doctors and dentists. One of them took a shine to me. And he showed it by forcing me to start investing.

Each morning he would find me and hand me the paper. Not the sports page, the money section. And he would say, "Airman Johns, this is the only part of the newspaper that matters, because with this section you can actually change your life. The politics page and the sports page won't change your life at all. But if you can get used to reading these investing stories, we can talk about them and I can teach you about stocks. You need to start by putting twenty-five dollars into a mutual fund."

I was so scared to do this that he promised to give me back my twenty-five dollars if I lost it in the stock market within six months. And of course I didn't. That was an unfounded fear.

But I still wasn't any good at putting the money away. I could see that—like eating my vegetables—it was a smart thing to do, but I had a hard time with it. And then, around my third year of service when I was going to night school and getting ready to finish my degree, he showed me something really interesting.

He had me look at the military pay grades. They're published every year, so even a lowly airman like I was could see what the brass were making.

"All right, Airman Johns," he said. "Listen up. If you stay in the military and you get to be a master sergeant, that's going to be worth about $5,000 a month to you, maybe $60,000 a year in twenty years, when you can start collecting your pension. That's the equivalent of a million dollars in the bank."

Because $1,000,000 drawing 6 percent interest—which is what a master sergeant would've gotten at the time—is about $60,000 a year. Does that make sense? To put it another way, $1,000,000 at 6 percent interest is the same as getting $60,000 a year in a pension.

"Now, I'll tell you, Airman Johns, that's a great deal. So if you're going to leave the military, finish school, and do something else, it had better be something that earns you more. You'll be in a race against time to make more than that by the time you would've retired from the military. Otherwise, why bother? Why leave? Just stick around and take that great pension."

Now *that* message landed hard. I'd always thought of the military as a means to an end. It was both my ticket to serve my country and a way to pay for college. On balance, I knew myself, and I was not cut out for that road, even if doing so meant a guaranteed financial future.

So I started sending that twenty-five-dollar check in to my mutual fund every damned month, like clockwork. Because now I had a little voice in my head saying, "I need to have at least a million dollars in the bank by the time I'm forty, or else I might as well have stayed in the military." I started early, I invested regularly, I read the financial section of the newspaper, I ate my veggies. And look at me now! Happy birthday to me. Bring on the cake, right?

Now that I've got you on board, let's dive into two other ways in addition to real estate that you can start investing and earning like a champ with the help of compound interest.

Compound Interest in the Stock Market

The average person tends to think that playing the stock market is incredibly risky. I'm writing this book in the middle of the COVID-19 crisis, and I've watched the market take a massive plunge, make a modest recovery, and continue to waver based on whatever is in the news that day. So, yeah, there's fluctuation and that means risk.

But—as many wise financial experts have said before me—that fluctuation is in the short term. If you begin investing in stocks early in your life and have the patience (and constitution) to keep it in the market for multiple decades, you will see your money grow. There's very little risk in most stock portfolios, especially if they're tied to indices like the S&P 500.

In case you're wondering, the S&P 500 is a stock market index that tracks the stocks of five hundred large-cap US companies. It does a decent job of reflecting the stock market's performance by reporting the risks and returns of some of the biggest companies including Microsoft, Amazon, and Apple. So performance is reported in the daily news, and investors use those numbers as a benchmark of the overall market.

But investment companies have also designed mutual funds to mimic the performance of market indices like the S&P 500. They've assembled portfolios of stocks and bonds that will provide broad market exposure, low operating expenses, and low portfolio turnover. All good things, and all ideal for first-time investors who want to dip a toe in the market and see how it feels. (Still leery? Warren Buffett has advised the trustee of his estate to put 90 percent of his cash into index funds.[10] Just sayin'.)

Newbie investors should also consider REITs, another toe-dipping option. REITs are companies that own, operate, or finance income-producing properties. Basically, they allow a bunch of investors to pool their money to invest in real estate assets. They come in several different flavors: some REITs buy properties and rent them to tenants; others develop properties from the ground up; and some focus on the mortgage and financial side of real estate without buying any properties at all.

REITs aren't exactly the same as traditional stocks, but most of them do trade on major stock exchanges, and they are even more stable than index funds. (Remember: Unless we all decide to move into caves, we will always need houses. Real estate is a solid investment.)

REITs allow lower-income investors to sink some money into real estate assets they couldn't afford on their own. Even if you can cobble together enough to buy a rental house, could you scrape up enough for a down payment on a high-rise office tower or a shopping mall? Probably not right this minute. With REITs, real estate dabblers can put money into billion-dollar commercial property portfolios with just a few hundred dollars to start.

What's that? You wanna know how all this ties back to compound interest? I'm getting there; keep your shirt on.

When you invest in the stock market, you will never earn a set interest rate. All that fluctuation makes that impossible. But the return you receive as an investor is based on the change in the value of your investment. When the value of your investment goes up, you earn a larger return.

Look at it this way: stock price is a reflection of the perceived value of a company. Companies that sell shares of themselves to investors make a profit (or "return") on those shares when the price of the stock rises. When this happens, the company reinvests some of that profit back into itself and, over time, that reinvestment makes a profit, too. Reinvestment makes the value, and therefore the stock price, compound. So it's not interest, exactly, but compound "growth," like in real estate.

Also, if you look at the entire stock market over long periods of time, you'll see behaviors that look similar to that of guaranteed compound interest. The investment grows slowly at first, then begins to pick up speed; then it starts to really soar once critical mass is reached. But with single stocks and shorter investment time frames, there's more risk, more volatility, and less of a chance that the soaring will actually take place.

Compound Interest in Boring Crap like CDs and Savings Accounts

What? I can be a jackass in this section if I want to.

Even if you know absolutely nothing about real estate or index funds, you undoubtedly understand that putting money into an interest-bearing savings account is a safe bet. Again, most of them pay utter crap for interest rates these days, and some offer simple interest rates instead of compounding ones, but there's nothing wrong with putting some of your cash into a savings account. (Just don't put it all in there.)

You may have only heard of CDs because your grandma gave you one for high school graduation, so I'll give you a quick overview. CD stands for certificate of deposit, which means you get a fancy piece of paper from a bank or credit union saying you agree to leave a lump-sum deposit untouched for a predetermined period of time in exchange for a kick-ass interest rate. Of course, "kick-ass" is relative. Since savings accounts are offering piddly little 0.7 percent rates, CDs sound super fabulous at 2 percent. Start with a huge deposit and leave it alone for a billion years, and your CD will work wonders. But if you only have a couple hundred to play with, you can make more on compounding growth elsewhere.

The $20,000 Couch

Some of you readers might be earning enviable salaries, even in your early twenties or thirties. Maybe you've got a swanky Silicon Valley job with a big ol' stock package, and you're starting to think about investing seriously. But first, you might as well set yourself up. You need a nice apartment and some slick furniture to deck it out, right?

So you cash out a little stock, go to Pottery Barn, and throw down $5,000 for a couch. After all, you've got a bunch of money. You've got a killer pad with a gorgeous view. You work hard and, damn it, you deserve this. You can't live in an apartment without furniture, so the $5,000 couch it is.

First off, cashing out is a truly terrible idea. To get that $5,000, you likely had to cash out $10,000 in stock. Stock that would've kept appreciating if you'd just left it alone. Second, think about how much that couch will be worth in one year. How much could you sell that swanky-ass $5,000 couch for just twelve months later?

$200, tops. Get on Craigslist and see for yourself.

That, friends, is called a depreciating asset. And your couch depreciated like gangbusters.

Now imagine your stock splits. Well, whaddya know. Now that $5,000 basically cost you $10,000. If you work at Google and your stock triples in value over two years, that stupid couch cost you a grand total of $20,000. Yes, it's true that you didn't actually spend $20,000 on it, but that's how much it *cost*. Because you yanked money out of a good investment vehicle and blew it on a bad idea. You bought stuff. A thing. An item. A marker of supposed wealth. And that is a losing proposition.

All of the millionaires I've ever met know that anything they buy will be worthless within a year—*except* their investments. They may buy antique coins or classic cars and hope for a teensy bit of appreciation, but when it comes to buying "stuff," they know it's equivalent to setting their money on fire. You need stuff to live, that's true. But you need wealth to become independent. You need investments that appreciate instead of depreciate. You need to think about how financial security will make you happy in the long term, instead of thinking about how happy a $5,000 Pottery Barn couch will make you in the short term.

Bottom line: You've gotta eat your vegetables.

Invest slowly, invest steadily, and be patient.

It won't be fun, but it *will* be profitable.

CHAPTER
6

Get a Money Mentor

YOU'VE ALREADY HEARD ME SAY that the myth of the self-made man is BS. Allow me to repeat myself: Millionaires do not earn their fortunes alone. Captains of industry do not rise to power solo. If you're serious about becoming a wildly successful investor who rakes in $10K every month, retires early, globe-hops, enjoys financial independence, and is busy Livin' La Vida Brady, you need a money mentor. Like, yesterday.

Here's why even seasoned investors and bona fide billionaires have and rely on money mentors: we don't know what we don't know. We all have blind spots, we all have weaknesses, and most of us aren't even aware they exist. Making tough or important decisions—especially financial ones—without objective input isn't just risky, it's downright dumb. A money mentor can see obstacles or issues you might completely fail to see, or even intentionally ignore. Even if you knew absolutely everything about passive income or real estate or whatever your investment vehicle of choice might be, you'd still make better choices with a mentor by your side.

But honestly? I also just think that people need to get into the habit of enrolling others in their visions. We shouldn't just hatch crazy plans for ourselves; we should enlist the help of people who've already executed similarly crazy plans so we've got a better shot at bringing our plans to fruition. We should show our commitment by asking for help and guidance from smart, seasoned experts.

Think about it this way: If you wanted to be a virtuoso oboe player, would you try to teach yourself all alone in your bedroom? If you wanted to be a tennis pro, would you skip hiring a coach and hit the ball against an office building by yourself? When we want to learn to do something right, we take lessons. We hire a teacher, work with them on an ongoing basis, and bring our questions to them so we can get perspective from someone wiser than ourselves.

There's no mechanism for learning about budgeting, earning, and investing in school, so why doesn't anyone take money lessons?

I think we should all start.

Brady's Money Mentor Sets Him Straight. Again.

I started at least twenty years ago.

I've had four financial mentors over the course of those two decades, and I can't tell you how many headaches and heartaches they've saved me. I learned early on that there's only so much you can learn from books. I'm not knocking books, obviously; I wrote this one that you're reading right now, so clearly I understand that they're important. But the thing is, you can't call up a book after a hard day and say, "I screwed this up. What do I do now?" You can't take a potential investment opportunity to a book and ask it what it thinks.

My money mentors have talked me down from ledges, talked me into buying houses I thought were worthless, talked me through some of the toughest moments in my life. But let's start with a relatively easy issue that smacked me in the face early on: a renter who wouldn't pay.

This was back in the college days, so Tom was the lucky stiff who was mentoring me at the time. For a couple of years running, I'd had responsible renters and no issues, but then I had a tenant who owed me three months of rent. And, silly as it may sound, I was stumped. I just couldn't fathom showing up on his doorstep, red-faced and filled with rage, to demand my money. And I couldn't imagine kicking him out. Even if I could, I didn't know how. But I was tending bar at the time, working my ass off and hard up for cash, and the mortgage was due. I needed that rent money to cover my expenses. So I called Tom and explained the situation and asked him what to do.

"I'll tell you what to do, you nitwit," he said affectionately. "Quit managing your own properties. You suck at it. Time to pay somebody else to take over."

"But I—"

"Lemme ask you something, Brady," Tom said. "Are you gonna be a manager or an investor?"

And I said, "Well, I'm gonna be an investor. But I got this property right now and the renter's not paying and you're not answering my question."

"Oh, I *am* answering your question. You need to pay professionals to do the things that you're bad at."

I was hopping mad at the idea of paying anyone anything, especially when I could do the work myself and pocket that money. But Tom kept at me.

"How much would a property manager get paid every month?"

I said, "Tom, you don't understand. What in the hell, man? I can't pay someone else right now!"

"You called me," he pointed out.

And that made me pause. My time in the military had taught me to shut off the rebellious voice in my head and listen to authority. To remind myself that, nine times out of ten, the person in charge is trying to help me. So I shut up and told him to go on.

Tom asked again, "How much would a property manager make every month?"

"I dunno," I said.

"Well, I do," he said. "Let's say $75 per month per property. If you're renting at $750 per month, that's 10 percent of the rent. Now, how much will you make bartending this weekend?"

"$200."

"Then why the hell are you on the phone arguing with me about a property manager who makes $75 a month?"

I was quiet.

"Your answer is to work another weekend if you need to pay that property manager," Tom said. "Your answer is to do the things that make the most money and hire someone to do the things that make the least money. Which also happens to be the things that you're not good at."

Fast-forward to the present for a moment, and I'll tell you that this conversation with Tom is the reason I've never mowed a single yard in my life. You know why? Because the professional property managers will always be better set up for success than I am. They've got better tools than

I do. Doing it frustrates the hell out of me, and it doesn't frustrate them one bit. Everybody's happy.

Okay, rewind back to the past.

"Fine, Tom, fine," I said, exasperated. "But what do I do right now? How do I find a property manager who can help me with this tenant?"

And he said, "You get off the phone with me, and you call my friend Jake. Tell him I sent you. He'll either handle it through his property management company or refer you to someone else who's just as good. Tell him you have a problem with a renter who's not paying, hand him this problem, and go back to doing what you do to make $200 in a single weekend."

Honestly, this was still not the answer I wanted. But because Tom was my mentor and I trusted him completely, I got off the phone, called his friend, and said, "I have an emergency."

Jake said, "Not really, you don't. I can handle that in twenty-four hours or less."

He told me what he was going to do, and then he did it, and it worked like a charm. And now I'm going to tell you, because you won't believe how simple and humane and fast the solution was. In a day, he fixed something I'd been agonizing over for three months.

Jake called my tenant and said, "Hey, I'm the new property manager and I understand you're behind on rent."

My tenant said, "Yeah, we'd love to pay it, but we just don't have the money."

(Side note: That was another embedded lesson for me in this situation. I was so busy thinking, "This jerk won't pay my rent," I never stopped to think, "Maybe this jerk *can't* pay my rent.")

So Jake said, "Okay, what if we rented you the U-Haul trailer and helped you find your next place. Could you be out in forty-eight hours?"

"I'm not sure," the tenant said.

"What if we paid you $100 to move?" Jake asked.

"Then I'll get right out."

Remember, I'd be making $200 that weekend. So $100 went to the tenant, fifty to the U-Haul rental, and seventy-five to Jake. I was out twenty-five dollars on the deal, but by Monday I had a new renter in there who could pay the rent.

I've never managed a single property since.

And I probably wouldn't have been able to come up with that solution on my own. Without Tom's advice and insight, without him being a truth teller for me, I would've wrung my hands and continued to lose money for God knows how long. Tom didn't tell me what I wanted to hear, but he told me what I needed to hear. He knew me, he knew my blind spots, and he forced me to look at the situation from a different angle. He gave me the gift of his own experience, and he saved me from myself.

Remember how I told you that my day job is in the tech world? Software developers like to say, "Emulate first, innovate second." In other words, think about copying someone before you think about inventing something totally new. Don't force yourself to build something from scratch when someone smarter has already created a solution. Don't struggle alone in the dark when you can ask someone with decades of experience. Don't guess. Ask your mentor. Copy your mentor. If you do, you might never have to do anything from scratch again.

How Will a Money Mentor Help You?

So now that you're super jealous of me for having such an amazing mentor, let's talk about you. You're newer to this than I am. You may have grown up in a different era and faced very different challenges throughout your life. How can I guarantee that connecting with a money mentor will benefit you personally? Couldn't you just get a business degree? Or work for an investment company and learn on the job?

Yeah, you could. And the fact is, you might get all you need from those experiences. But I sincerely doubt it, and here's why.

Mentorship will help you see that there's a difference between lack of effort and lack of talent. When you build a relationship with someone who already knows the stuff you want to know, they can shine a light on what you're good at. You, as an individual. They'll get to know you, observe you, watch you in action, and be able to offer real-time feedback in a way that a college professor or work supervisor seldom can. They'll be able to say, "If you put in more effort here, you'll get better. But this thing over here? You just don't have the talent for it. And that's fine. We can figure out another way to get it done." (Just like Tom did for me!)

A good mentor will show you that there is no secret to success. Most people succeed through a combination of trial and error and learning from others. They'll teach you to copy first, invent second. They'll save you from wasting your time, show you valuable shortcuts, and praise your efforts. Investing is like anything else; it has a learning curve. When you're paired with a money mentor, you'll have someone by your side who will keep you from getting frustrated and remind you that everyone else went through this same painful process.

Working with a mentor will help you get a financial education you cannot possibly get in school. Nope, not even business school. You can have an MBA from Harvard and still learn tips and tricks from a money mentor. Why? Because of all that trial and error. School is theory; mentorship is practice.

Finally, doing hard shit alone is the worst. Learning to be an investor, and then learning to be a great investor, and then figuring out how to manage your fast-growing fortune will be hard. Your money mentor will make it less stressful, less confusing, and less lonely.

Convinced? Good. Now let's work on finding your perfect mentor.

How to Find a Money Mentor

I'm not going to lie to you, finding a mentor can be tough. Smart, accomplished, wealthy people get lots of requests for their time and help, which means that being approached by some random person who needs a mentor may just irritate them. So you've got to go about this strategically.

Start by researching formal mentorship programs in your area. The easiest way to hook up with a dedicated mentor is to connect with an organization that has a giant roster of smart people looking for mentees. If your town or region doesn't have a local mentoring program, there are national organizations like mentoring.org and findamentor.com that can point you in the right direction.

If you have your sights set on a specific person as your money mentor—say, a local luminary or a finance writer (or me)—don't just contact them out of the blue. If they give talks or host seminars, show up and introduce yourself a few times. Connect with them on LinkedIn. Ask around within your own network and see if anyone could make a personal connection. Interact with them on social media. Basically, stalk them in every way that's both possible and legal to get yourself on their radar before making the ask. Mentoring can be a whopper of a commitment, so you want to prove that you're serious and an actual follower of their work.

If you have no idea who would be your perfect mentor, you've got a tougher road ahead of you, but that doesn't mean you shouldn't commit to walking it. And since I've cajoled total strangers into mentoring me multiple times, I've got some tips for you. Ready?

- **Offer to pay:** This is tip number one for a reason, people. If you're going to approach some wildly successful person and ask them to be your go-to when you're in a financial bind, you need to make it worth their while. And you need to show them you respect them and won't waste their time or yours on this mentorship. You don't want advice you can get for free anyway. You want the good stuff from someone who is already financially independent. So offer to pay. Say something like, "Listen, I have no idea what an hour of your time is worth, but I certainly don't want to ask you to do this for free. Can we discuss a way to compensate you for the time we spend together?" When you ask graciously, you may find that they don't want money anyway, but they may want something else like your help or expertise. But don't expect that. Expect to pay. It'll be worth it.

- **Ask around:** Start with your family, friends, coworkers, professors, and neighbors. Say that you're working on taking ownership of your financial future and are looking for a money mentor. Do they know anyone who is financially independent? Anyone who loves real estate or the stock market? Ideally someone who's relatively friendly and potentially open to taking on a young whippersnapper as a mentee?

- **Look for someone older than you:** I know, I know. There are plenty of young investors who've already made a fortune. But I've had multiple real estate mentors over the years, and they've all been about twenty years older than I am. The best ones are always at least twenty years older because that means they've experienced two financial eras that you haven't. They've lived through crashes and crises, bounced back, and come out on top.

- **Make sure they're the real deal:** I'm not saying that you need to hire a private investigator or anything, but before you go offering some rando a bunch of money to give you advice, do some digging. Make sure they acquired that money through expertise, not inheritance or luck or something worse. You know what I'm saying? And on top of that, you don't want someone who isn't financially independent telling you about money. Do your homework to make sure you're working with someone who truly does know how to save and invest.

- **Set timelines and parameters:** How often do you want to meet? How long will each meeting last? What are your goals? Will you send an agenda or questions ahead of time for your mentor to review and prepare? Offering details like these up front shows that you're serious and won't waste anyone's precious time.

Last thing? Know what you want as a mentee. You don't have to have a ten-year plan sketched out, but you do have to go into the relationship knowing what kind of advice and guidance you need. Do you want to know more about investing in start-up businesses? Do you want to buy and rent houses? Do you need help zeroing out your debt *and* figuring out how to save and invest at the same time? Know your goals and know your situation so that when you reach out to your potential mentor, you can say exactly why they're the right person to guide you. Tell them what it is about their knowledge or background that makes them a good fit, and explain what you're hoping to gain.

The Suit, the Promissory Note, and the Monthly BBQ Deliveries

As it happens, I can also tell you how *not* to approach a potential money mentor. I acquired this unfortunate wisdom from personal experience—shocker, I know—but luckily, it came with a pretty fantastic story.

So, back in the early days, there was a craptastic dilapidated house on the outskirts of Austin that I had my heart set on. I'd already bought a few properties by this time, had already taken Tom's advice to bring in a professional property manager, and was thoroughly convinced I was hot shit. I identified this house as my next one, found out the man who owned it had also built it, and tracked him down.

This was no mean feat, for two reasons. One is that the house was not for sale. But, you see, one of those Brady things is that I'd much rather buy a house before it goes up for sale so I don't have to pay the real estate agent fees. Save myself 6 percent. And the truth was I couldn't pay those fees at the time anyway. If I did, I wouldn't have enough left to fix the place up so that I could actually rent it.

The other thing is that there was no internet back then, so I had to haul my ass out to the courthouse in San Marcos, Texas, and rummage through a stack of books to find the property listing that told me who the owner was. Then I had to go to the phone books—something most of you fine readers have never seen—and try to find out where this guy lived. Lucky for me, he lived right there in Austin.

His name was Trigg Forister, and when I called his development office, I discovered he had a voice like molasses dripping off a tin roof. I am telling you, this was the most southern guy I'd ever encountered in my life. Anyway, I called him up and I said, "Mr. Forister, I'm Brady Johns. We don't know each other, but I'm wondering if I can talk to you about buying the house at this address."

And he said, "Yes, you can come by my office."

So I went by his office. I came straight from the barbecue restaurant where I'd just finished my shift, so I smelled like meat and smoke and sugar. I'd put on the only suit that I had, because I knew businesspeople wore suits all the time. I hated that, but I did it. And I drove down to his office in my hilariously ancient Jetta that had three hundred thousand miles on it and was being held together with paper clips and chewing gum. The air conditioner was broken and it was July and I was wearing a cheap suit. So I was hot and grouchy.

I walked into Trigg Forister's office, and he was sitting at a massive oak desk surrounded by an absolute tornado of Texas memorabilia, including about a dozen state flags and a set of longhorns over his head. He was seventy years old or so, and he had an air of amused patience about him. Which I decided to decimate.

I had my pitch down. I'd read all these real estate books written by total assholes who claimed that you could never negotiate, that you could demand anything you wanted, that you should never take the first deal you're offered. Oh, and the best one? The first person to mention a price loses the negotiation. I mean, these books were packed cover to cover with bad advice, and I'd eaten them up.

So I waltzed into his office—sweaty, smelling of barbecue, and with a head full of dumbfuckery—and I said, "Mr. Forister, I'm Brady Johns and I'm here to buy that house from you."

He looked at me and cocked his head a little. He said, "How are you going to pay for this house, son?"

I said, "Well, I just got out of the military and I'm working over at Green Mesquite."

"Green Mesquite?" he said. "I love Green Mesquite."

"Well, yeah, I'm working over there and maybe one day I can buy it," I declared. Like an idiot. "But right now I've saved up $500, and if you'll let me buy your property with no money down, I can put the $500 back into the house. I can give you that money as the down payment, but I think it's just better if I can put it toward improving the property."

So I'm spelling it out for him, right? This man who was more than forty years older and understood the real estate game back to front. Then he leaned back in his chair in his starched shirt and pressed blue jeans and looked at me. Hard.

"Where'd you grow up?" he asked, changing the subject.

"Well, I grew up in Gainesville, Texas, and I worked cattle when I was a boy."

"I figured you worked cattle growing up," he said.

And I said, "Okay."

I was confused and a little annoyed. What was this guy doing? What did it matter where I'd grown up? I was here to do business, dammit, not make friends.

What I failed to realize was that being friends, or at least being friendly, was how this man did business. So I put the pedal to the metal.

"Here's how I'm going to buy this house," I told him. "I'm not putting any money down."

And he said, "Now, I think you're a little out of line on how much that house is worth. I think it's worth a little more than you're offering."

"No, it's not."

"Okay. I'm going to be nice to you and tell you to get the hell out of my office. Right now," he said. "And I'm not going to tell you twice."

When he said that in that sweet southern drawl, I knew I'd blown it. I tucked tail and hustled right out of his office.

Later that day, I met up with my mentor Tom.

"Well, how'd it go with the Mr. Forister?" he asked.

"He doesn't get it," I said. "I went in there, I told him I wanted to buy the house with no money down, and he just kicked me out of his office."

I told Tom about the office itself and how Mr. Forister had asked me all sorts of dumb questions about my upbringing. I told him all this in exasperation while dripping sweat onto his driveway.

Tom took a moment to size me up. Then he said, "Did you go over there in that suit?"

And I said, "Yeah."

"Huh. All right. And you told him that?"

"Yeah!" I said. "Because the first person who mentions the price loses."

Tom shook his head and looked at the ground for a moment.

"First of all," he said, "I've never met Mr. Forister but I know who he is. He's pretty well-respected around here. He's probably got $100 million in the bank and I can't even figure out why he took your call."

My jaw dropped. "No shit?"

"No shit," Tom said. "Brady, listen, that man could actually help you fix up your life. You know why he was getting all personal with you? He saw something in you that he liked about himself. You went through all this trouble to go find him, which took a lot of initiative and showed him that you don't mind hard work. But then you just charged in there and insulted the man by telling him what he was going to do with his property."

I was silent. But I knew Tom was right.

"Here's my advice," he said. "You've got to go to Green Mesquite later, right?"

I did.

"All right. Why don't you go now, go put on your Green Mesquite shorts and your T-shirt and go pick up a couple of pounds of barbecue and go back over to Mr. Forister's office. See if he'll let you far enough into the door to apologize and hand him that barbecue. Then you tell him you just fucked everything up and that you're sorry."

"Why would he let me in, though?"

"You ever go over to somebody's house and their dog comes running up to you all happy and barking? And you walk up to that dog and it rolls right over and you know that dog would let you pat its belly and be your friend for the rest of its life?"

I said, "Yeah. What's that got to do with it?"

"Son, nobody kicks a puppy in the belly when that puppy rolls over," Tom told me. "Now, you need to go get Mr. Forister some barbecue, show him you're a workingman, and apologize. Just you go over there and tell him you recognize you did something wrong."

I screwed up my courage, went and got some barbecue, put on my shorts and my work boots, and drove back over to Trigg Forister's office in my shitty Jetta. I knocked on the door of his office, and when it opened, I just thrust the bag through. I'd actually written "Sorry" right there on the bag.

But his secretary was the one who'd opened the door, and she said, "Come on in. Let me take that barbecue in there, and I'll see if he's busy." And she came back out directly and told me, "Go on in. He'll see you."

And so I walked in, and all in one big rush I said, "Mr. Forister, I'm working two jobs right now. I'm also going to school and I'll graduate next year and I've got $500 and I was just trying to be as tall as you are."

After a pause he said, "All that true?"

"Yes it is, sir."

"You really work cattle growing up?"

"Yes, I did."

"Me, too."

And he started telling me about his own life.

I sat and we talked about growing up around cattle, and how farming had changed, and what we loved about Texas. He told me how he'd gotten started in real estate, and how long he'd been a one-man shop, and all sorts of other things about his personal history. And this time, I listened. I was respectful and patient.

After a while, he said, "I've got to tell you the truth. I forgot I even owned that house. I got willed that house by an aunt who died, but I never really think about it!"

And that's how rich Trigg Forister was. That house was not rented, but it could've been if he'd fixed it up. Or he could've sold it ages ago. But he was doing so well he'd completely forgotten about a valuable asset he had sitting vacant.

He sold it to me with no money down and told me to sink my $500 into repairs. After that, every time I had to make a payment, I drove over to his office with barbecue. Every damned month. The barbecue didn't cost me much, and bringing it was really just an excuse to hear one more story from Trigg.

Tom had been right. Nobody wants to kick a puppy in the belly, do they? And you're always better off being honest from the beginning, whether you're asking someone for a deal, or their help, or their ongoing guidance and mentorship. Building relationships is about finding points of connection, shared experiences. So, if someone who might be able to mentor you decides to tell you stories about their life or ask you questions about yours, respect that. Let it unfold. You can learn an awful lot from spreadsheets and stock tips, but you can learn an awful lot more from the stories people share with you.

Never Stop Learning

A couple of years ago, I decided I wanted to talk with Jimmy Buffett. I've always loved his music and, just like Chris Blackwell, whom you met in the introduction, he seemed to be living the type of life I truly wanted for myself. I worked a little networking magic, got his email address from a buddy, and offered to give $10,000 to his favorite charity if he'd spend an hour talking with me. I won't share the details of that conversation with you, because they're none of your damned business, but I will say that it was enlightening, fun, and totally worth the ten-large.

Did that hour of time count as mentorship? It sure as hell did. Mentorship can last a lifetime or it can last a day. It all depends on what you want to get out of it, the volume and specificity of the advice you're seeking. With Jimmy Buffett, I was X years old and I wanted Y. With Tom, I was much younger and needed a longer commitment and broader knowledge. But both were mentors to me. Both played a role in my financial education.

And now I mentor others. I've found that once you're in a position of power or knowledge, you genuinely want to help others when you can. Smart, confident people just tend to feel this way. It feels good to advise and support those coming up behind you because you remember how it felt to be them. You remember how lost and overwhelmed you were when you first got started, and you want to make it just a little bit easier for the next generation.

All right, before I get all misty-eyed talking about "you young people," I'll quit. But let me say this bit one last time: you—yes, you—need a money mentor. So make a plan, find a likely candidate, and ask for their help humbly and sincerely. Bring them barbecue. It'll be the best thing you ever do for your financial well-being.

CHAPTER
7

Borrowing Money When You're Broke

ARE YOU READY FOR A story about filthy rich Texas oilmen with outsized personalities? Of course you are.

Back in the early 1940s, H. L. Hunt was in his prime and gambling like a fiend. He played poker constantly and had traded some of his winnings for oil rights, ultimately securing the title to a huge chunk of the East Texas Oil Field, which just happened to have some of the world's largest oil deposits. So the dude was loaded. As in he could lose $30,000 in a single night of Texas Hold'em and not even flinch.[11] (In 1957, he was worth around $600 million. That's $5.6 billion in twenty-first-century dollars. Oh, and his house on White Rock Lake in Dallas was built to look like Mount Vernon, but way bigger. So this was not a guy who shied away from conspicuous consumption.)

During the big oil strike days, he liked to gather up some of the wealthiest men in Texas and sit them down to a poker game. While they were playing, ol' H. L. would force them to talk about big ideas or, at the very least, he'd make them offer their opinions on interesting questions. Things like, "Who's your hero?" or "What's your worst trait?" or "Do you have a personal motto?"

One night, the topic of the conversation was, "What's the greatest invention in human history?" Now remember, these people had seen penicillin get discovered. They'd seen the invention of cars, and a few had even seen the first manned aircraft take flight. They went around the table calling out inventions like the light bulb and the telephone, but when it came to H. L.'s turn, know what he said?

The promissory note. This obscenely rich oil baron believed the promissory note was mankind's greatest invention.

So what the hell is a promissory note? It's a type of informal credit, and later in this fabulous chapter, we'll talk definitions, guidelines, and all the best ways to make these notes work for you as a budding investor.

But right now, we're going to spend some time dispelling the myths that credit only comes from banks and that utilizing credit is some form of financial weakness. Because both of those notions are Grade A bullshit. Credit can exist between two people who trust each other. Credit can be negotiated on whatever terms the lender and recipient believe to be fair. And credit is just a tool, something that can be used to make financial activities and expenditures possible. It's not good or bad; it's totally neutral. And guess what? Every financially independent person in the world uses it.

Borrowing Money Is Totally Normal

Let's forget about straight investment for a sec and talk about business. Do you think Nathan Blecharczyk, Brian Chesky, and Joe Gebbia founded Airbnb using just the money in their own piggy banks? Do you think Arianna Huffington built her media empire on her own savings? Do you think Elon Musk used his own cash to launch Tesla? Hell no, they didn't.

Businesses usually get started when a person has an idea and borrows money to turn that idea into a product. They might borrow from a bank, but they might just as easily borrow from a friend or a family member or an angel investor. And the borrowing might happen with gobs of interest and collateral, or none of either. Borrowing money is a normal part of starting a business, and you can do it in a wide variety of ways.

Believe me when I tell you that everybody who ever got rich did it by borrowing money at some point. They made it worthwhile for their lenders, and eventually they paid it all back, but they didn't fund all of their investments and business endeavors from scratch. They had help. They borrowed. In fact, if you flip back to the introduction of this book, you'll see that someone a hell of a lot wealthier than I am once suggested that I should be borrowing more money more often!

Before we get too far into this chapter, I need to hit you with a short list of things that I am not going to recommend you do.

1. I am *not* going to recommend that you borrow money for no reason.
2. I am *not* going to recommend that you borrow money and never pay it back.

3. I am *not* going to recommend that you borrow money from someone who cannot afford to lend it. Or who doesn't want to lend it.

4. I am *not* going to recommend that you borrow money without understanding all of the terms of the loan.

5. And I am *not* going to recommend that you borrow money without having a solid plan for how and when you'll pay it back.

So while you'll hear me describing the wonders of promissory notes with glee, do not mistake that glee for blanket permission to start borrowing from everyone you know willy-nilly. Promissory notes are easy, simple, and wonderful tools for investment, but they are also legally binding agreements. Do not use them to snow your friends out of their hard-earned cash and then force those friends to drag your ass to court.

Borrowing money is normal, and it can be incredibly beneficial. But only if you use your common sense when you do it.

Borrowing Money from People, Not Banks

I've already shared several stories in which I used promissory notes to make real estate deals. This is, in essence, borrowing money from individual people instead of from banks. If I ever needed a down payment for a property and was short on cash, I would borrow money more directly from people in my life using promissory notes. No banks involved. If this sounds insane or hilariously risky to you, consider the following.

When some clever MIT grads cook up an idea that will become the next big app, they seek angel investors. These private investors have an abundance of liquid money and an interest in putting it toward interesting projects. They typically hear a pitch from the budding entrepreneurs and then agree to invest a certain sum of money in exchange for owner-ship equity in the company. No banks involved.

Ever heard of a hedge fund? Of course you have. But you might not be 100 percent sure what one is. (No judgment here! I had no clue either until I was at least thirty-five.) Basically, a bunch of wealthy investors get together, form a little partnership, pool their funds, and create a small business that operates as a limited liability corporation with the goal of investing their money as a unit. They use methods that are considered high-risk—including investing with borrowed money—in hopes of mak-ing even more money. Banks may be involved in holding the cash for individual investors, but they are not involved in the hedge fund partner-ship itself.

How about private equity? Another fancy term that just sounds like rich folks' business to most of us. Private equity means buying into a company that doesn't sell shares on a stock exchange. Although this can mean a rich person sinking money into a scrappy start-up, it's more likely to play out as rich people loaning money to other rich people to do big, rich things. And guess what? The investor gives the money directly to the company in exchange for partial ownership or a promise of payback. No banks involved.

Banks have their charms. (They also have their downsides, as we'll discuss.) But they are far from your only option when it comes to drum-ming up investment funds. People have been borrowing money from each other for millennia, long before the first bank opened its doors. And one of the advantages of borrowing from individuals is that it forces you to enroll other people in your idea before you get started. It lets you practice at negotiating and helps you hone your pitch, but even more importantly, it puts you in a position where you have to prove you're passionate and dedicated to making this investment work. If you can't convince another person you're in it to win it, then what the hell are you doing anyway?

As I've said many times before, if you want to become independently wealthy, you won't be able to do it alone. You will need help. And investors = help.

Banks Are Stores That Sell Money

A few years ago, my wife and I got into a situation where we needed to borrow some money. Don't laugh, it happens. Even to investment wonks like me. We were in a bind to the tune of needing $100,000 in a pinch, so naturally, I called up my bank and said, "Hey there, bank, I gotta borrow a hundred grand, and I'd like to borrow it against my properties."

Now, remember that, with all of my investment properties, I've got a sizable net worth. I mean, $100,000 didn't even scratch the surface. I just needed it in cash, and quickly. And I had worked with my bank on hundreds of deals over the years, so I called them up, fully expecting them to say, "No problem, Mr. Johns, come right over and we'll cut you a check."

What I got instead was, "Well, no. We just can't do that."

So what did I do? I got indignant. I read 'em the riot act with lots of "I've brought your bank all sorts of business" and "You call this customer service?" type stuff (and probably some deeply unprofessional swearing thrown in for good measure). I was hopping mad that they'd deny me a loan when I was really hurting and needed their help.

About an hour after the riot act reading was done, my banker called me up and asked to take me to lunch. And he gave me a peek behind the curtain.

"Hey, you know, this isn't our fault, right?" he said. "I mean, don't get pissed off again, but we really can't do this deal for you right now. Not because of you, obviously, but because we've loaned out a whole bunch of money and we literally don't have any more to lend for two weeks, based on our limits."

"Are you serious?"

"Deadly," he said. "If you really want this, can you wait two weeks? We will absolutely get it to you then."

And I appreciated the man's honesty, so I said, "Sure, sure."

But within ten seconds, my brain was whirring away in my skull, brimming with questions.

"Hang on," I said. "Do all banks work like this? With lending limits?"

And he said, "Yeah, we all work like this. It's a federal standard. We can only loan out a certain amount of money in a certain amount of time."

Some of you may already be saying, "Duh, Brady, everyone knows that," but lemme tell you it was news to me. Me! Someone who'd been borrowing money for twenty years. So I'm sharing it with you now in case, like me, you had no clue that banks could burn through their available lending cash and end up with their hands tied for weeks at a time.

So, after lunch, what did I do? I whipped out my cell and called my mentor.

"How did I not know this?" I demanded. "That banks have limits? That *my* bank might not have money to lend me when I really need it?"

"Oh yeah, I've been through this rigamarole," he said. "You need to call up a bank that's only got one branch in a small town."

"What? Why?"

"Because they don't have any customers like you," he said. "They're used to dealing with folks who need a couple thousand dollars because they're behind on rent. Look up a one- to two-branch bank that you've never heard of before, and they're going to have the same lending standards as your regular bank, but they won't have as many customers."

So I went back to work and I picked up the phone and called some random small bank.

I said, "Hey, I'm Brady Johns and I need to speak to somebody who can loan a hundred grand at a time because I've got to borrow a hundred grand."

Do you see what I did there? I embedded lesson number two in that little snippet of dialogue. Because the other thing my mentor revealed during our call is that some bankers have higher lending limits than others. If you hit a wall with one, ask for another. Or just start the whole transaction by making sure you're talking to someone who can actually cut you the deal you need.

Why be so blunt? Because, my good people, banks are stores that sell money. They want you to borrow from them because, when you do, they make money. They make interest on your loan. So if you need to borrow $100,000 and get saddled with Banker Phil who has a $50,000 lending limit, is he going to send you over to Banker Maria who can get you what you need? Hell no. There is a good chance that Banker Phil will just tell you no, he can't make your loan happen, without bothering to explain that his colleague can loan you more.

So if you talk to someone and they say no, I'm telling you, you need to ask them if they have the authority to loan that kind of money. Just like my mentor made me do.

When he first laid that bit of info on me, I said, "I don't know, man. I talked to my own banker. I've known the people at my bank a long time, and I don't really wanna do an end run around them." I gave him every excuse in the book.

"How bad do you need this money?" he asked.

I said, "Real bad."

"Well, then, fuck your friendship," he said. "This isn't about friendship. You can keep borrowing money from your original bank, too. Just because you're taking this one loan elsewhere doesn't mean you have to abandon your bank for good."

Think of going to a store and trying on four shirts, or four skirts, or whatever it is you're buying. Now think of going to multiple stores and trying on multiple garments before finding the right fit. Borrowing from banks is the same thing, if you decide to go the bank route at all. You may need to go to four banks and just keep asking until you connect with the right person, or find a bank that hasn't burned through its lending limit. Be persistent and shop around.

And for the love of all that's holy, never think of a bank as "your" bank. Banks love for us to talk that way, to be blindly loyal to them, because it's just a hell of a lot easier. But the Fourteenth National Bank of East Goatrope is not "your" bank. You don't own it. And you don't owe it anything. It's an institution. It's a money store. Just because a bank wants you to borrow from it, that doesn't mean you have one iota of obligation to do so.

In fact, you don't have to borrow money from a bank at all.

Appreciate, Don't Depreciate

And regardless of where your borrowed money comes from, I need you to promise me that you won't use it to purchase depreciating assets. Ever. Because if you do, I will hunt you down and give you a stern talking-to that you will never forget.

Quick refresher: Depreciating assets are things you sink money into that decrease in value over time, or that have no resale value whatsoever once they are purchased. You've heard the one about how new cars lose 20 percent of their value the second you drive them off the lot, right? That's depreciation in the extreme. You could probably guess that other vehicles like boats and motorcycles also plummet in value once they're purchased. Less obvious examples include clothing, computers, travel expenses, and sporting equipment—or that $20,000 couch. Basically, it's anything that sucks up your money and gives you an object or experience in return.

As you might've guessed, appreciating assets increase in value over time. The obvious ones are stocks, bonds, mutual funds, and real estate. Assets like jewelry (especially gold), antiques, artwork, sports memorabilia, and musical instruments may also appreciate, but you can't bank on them gaining steady value. It gets a little trickier when you consider stuff like home renovations; if the work you do increases the sale value of the home, that's a tangential form of appreciation. If it doesn't, you've set your money on fire.

That said, I'd rather see you borrow a boatload of money to fix up your house—or a rental property you've purchased—than spend that loan money on a fancy watch or a trip to Paris. And that goes for the "borrowing" that happens when you use credit cards, too. I'm always surprised when I see people put plane tickets and expensive gifts on their credit cards, which amounts to borrowing those funds at an exorbitant interest rate, then balk at the idea of borrowing the same amount of money so they can sink it into real estate or stocks. What's wrong with borrowing some money to go buy stocks as long as you're going to hold the stock? You're going to have to pay it off one way or the other.

Summary of this little rant: I'm all for people borrowing money for any asset that appreciates. But like any investor worth their salt, I am dead set against borrowing money for depreciating assets.

The Payback Money Doesn't Care Where It Came From

You've borrowed some money to invest. You either shopped it around to several banks, or you found some people in your life who were willing to back your investment personally. You got the funds, and you made the investment. Now you just need to wait until the investment brings in a bunch of returns, and you can pay back your lenders, right?

No, friends. That is not how paying down borrowed money works.

I see it constantly, though. New real estate investors borrow what they need, buy rental properties, and then cling to the belief that only the real estate itself can pay off their loans. I didn't do that. I borrowed money all over the place and paid it off as fast as I could using whatever money I earned from my jobs and investments. In fact, paying down my promissory notes is one of the reasons I worked two jobs all those years. I had no intention of using the sad little trickle of income I got from rent money to pay down my debts. Hell no! I wanted to be square as fast as possible, and that meant using earned money to pay off borrowed money.

Obviously, you have to come up with the money to pay your investors from somewhere, but as my mom used to say, "The money doesn't care where it comes from."

Money may not have feelings, but your investors do. And if you don't pay them back in a timely manner and under your agreed-upon terms, those feelings will turn ugly. To state the painfully obvious truth, you have to pay it all back. You just do. And that means enrolling others in your idea is the first step, and creating a solid, practical strategy for paying them back is the second.

Need a place to start? Here are some simple payback strategies that can work with banks just as well as they work with promissory notes. Your very first step is calculating the total amount you'll owe based on the term (time period) of the loan and the interest rate. So, if you borrow $1,000 over a ten-year period with an interest rate of 10 percent per year, the total amount you're really borrowing is $2,000. Use *that* number when you're creating a payment plan. Then consider these options:

1. Dedicate a percentage of your take-home pay to paying down your debts.
2. Allot a certain amount of money every week or month toward paying off your promissory notes and loans.
3. Save money automatically and in small ways, either through setting up automatic transfers from your checking account to a savings account or utilizing one of the many fantastic micro-investing apps, like Acorns. (These strategies work best as supplements, not as your sole strategy!)
4. Get a part-time job or side gig and put all of that money toward your debts.
5. Make extra payments any time you get a windfall.

There are infinite ways to pay back a loan, even if that loan is large and long term. Don't believe that if you borrow money for an investment, the investment itself is the only way to pay it back. Absolutely no one involved in the transaction cares where the payback money comes from.

But you *must* pay back your lenders. So, before you borrow a dime, decide how you're going to pay it back.

How to Make a Promissory Note

The absolute simplest way to borrow money in a legal, official, stands-up-in-court way is to use a promissory note. This credit vehicle gets its name because it is a written *promise* to repay a set amount of money by an agreed-upon date, though some people just call them personal loans. Now, I've hinted at these agreements in previous chapters, but this is where we're gonna dig into the nitty-gritty of 'em so you can decide if you want to use them yourself.

Years ago, you'd need to work with an attorney to set up a promissory note, but now? You can literally download templates from the internet. I mean, you can actually write something up on a cocktail napkin and most judges will consider it legal tender, but my lawyer would prefer that I point you toward the downloadable template. They're safer, more thorough, and less likely to end in tears.

Now, one of the reasons I love promissory notes as much as our pal Mr. Hunt did is that they often set up terms that include interest but no collateral. The interest makes it worthwhile for the lender to hand you a chunk of change and wait a long time to get it back. But lack of collateral means that if you fink out, that lender can't come after your paychecks or car or that chest of gold doubloons you've got buried under the garage. Lack of collateral means you can borrow money without having money. It means your lender trusts you enough to believe you'll pay them back, even if you don't have hard evidence of it right now in the form of material wealth.

Add this as another piece of evidence for my case that you don't have to *have* money to *make* money.

My main cautions about promissory notes have already been well covered in this chapter, but just in case you've been skimming: use whatever terms you want as long as they're agreeable to both parties, and don't borrow without having a payback plan already in place. Simple as that.

So, whom should you approach about promissory lending? This is where you'll need to get a little gregarious.

Talk to a few people in your work life, in your family, among your social circles, sports groups, or religious groups. Tell them what you're trying to do, whether it's build a stock portfolio, learn how to be a real estate investor, or become a professional tiger trainer. Let them know you're looking to borrow money, since you can't fund the whole thing yourself. Now here's the crucial part: When you talk to folks, tell them, "If you're not interested or able to contribute personally, do you know any people who loan money like this and would be?"

My lawyer won't let me say that I guarantee someone will have a connection for you, but secretly, I *do* guarantee it. Because we all know someone with a bit of cash, or we know someone who knows someone. If you commit to having three to five of these casual conversations about your financial plans, you will shake loose an investor or two.

And listen, don't be shy about hitting up your family members. I can't tell you how many stories I've heard about grandmas giving seed money to Silicon Valley start-ups and quietly becoming millionaires. People want to be a part of a dream. They want in. They want to support folks who are being bold and who are proactively planning for their own futures. Especially if they happen to be related to those folks.

On the flip side, be aware that some people either don't have the ability to invest or aren't comfortable sharing details about their own financial standing. In the first case, believe them and don't push. Take no for an answer and walk away. In the second case, same deal; don't push, don't press, don't fight them. It doesn't matter why they aren't willing to loan you money; it only matters that they just don't want to do it. And you never want to borrow money from somebody who didn't want to give it to you in the first place.

But finding the people who are all too eager to sign on to your investment dream is a cinch, I swear. So, even if you're not 100 percent ready to start buying houses or stocks, I'm going to give you a homework assignment: over the next week or so, when you're with a group of friends or chatting with coworkers, start floating the idea. You don't even have to say the loan is for you! Just say, "Hey, you know what? I met this guy who's looking to borrow money for a business that he's starting up, and he's not going to be able to get a lot of bank money. So he's wondering about private investors and people that wouldn't mind making money by creating personal loans. Do you know anyone who does that?"

Watch what comes back to you. Somebody is bound to say, "Hey, you know, I'd be interested in that. How much do they need?" Soon you've got $1,000, $2,000 available to you. Then somebody else chimes in with, "I've got a cousin. They've done this before. Let me get you their info."

Watch what happens. You already know your investors. I guarantee it. (Just don't tell my lawyer.)

It Doesn't Take Money to Make Money

If you're broke or darned near it right now, that's okay. Whenever people tell me, "I don't have any money," I say, "Well, congratulations. At least you know where you are and you're not hiding from it. That's more than most people can say." And then I talk to them about their dreams and goals, and the types of investments that excite them. I forbid them from putting anything on a credit card ever again, and I introduce them to mankind's greatest invention, the promissory note. I tell them rich people borrow money all the damned time, and that it's perfectly okay to borrow if you're smart enough and dedicated enough to pay it all back on time.

I basically tell them the entire contents of this chapter. So, if you're broke and you've skipped to the end here, go back. Reread. Find out how easy it is to borrow money, even if you don't have any of your own.

CHAPTER
8

Start (or Invest in) a Business

I DON'T CONSIDER MYSELF AN entrepreneur. I've done plenty of business deals and have a solid understanding of how the corporate world functions, but I've never come up with an idea or cultivated a skill I believed I could market. So why am I including a chapter in this book on launching your own business?

Because back in chapter four I told you there are three basic ways to make a healthy nonpaycheck income:

1. Investing in stocks, bonds, and markets
2. Creating or investing in a business
3. Investing in real estate

Although I'm far too lazy to launch a business myself, there's no denying that doing so can help you build your wealth in effective and engaging ways. And I'll admit to investing in a few businesses myself—namely, restaurants. I may not be brave (or is it foolish?) enough to try building a new eatery from scratch, but I've happily sunk some capital into a few Austin restaurants that are near and dear to me, including the Green Mesquite barbecue place where I worked all through college. So I've had a peek behind the curtain of entrepreneurship, even if the blood, sweat, and tears belonged to someone else.

The point I'm trying to make is that creating or investing in businesses may not be my personal favorite way to make money, but it's legit, it's exciting, and it'll give you a great opportunity to learn about yourself. Remember how I encouraged you to enroll other people in your investment ideas? Well, launching your own business gives you another opportunity to practice that skill. And sinking money into existing startups is the absolute best way to help other people bring their ideas to life (and to market). Both of these routes can be insanely risky or laughably humdrum—depending on the flavor of business you happen to pick—but both will also teach you a ton about hard work, cultivating professional relationships, and how to build a complex endeavor from scratch.

So what I'm saying is this: launching, investing in, or buying businesses should be on your radar as investment avenues. When you close your eyes and picture the future version of yourself who's financially independent and as happy as a pig in shit, I don't want you to tailor that vision to passive income sources alone.

Many of you were born to invent apps and improve systems, or scout out brilliant businesses and help them take over new markets. And to state the obvious, there are truckloads of money to be made in business-building and venture capitalism. So even though I'm a non-entrepreneur (or a non-trepreneur, if you will), I still want to give you the high-level overview. If you're hungry for details, you can check out the reading list at the end of this chapter.

Sound good? Awesome.

But First—a Minor Rant About Side Hustles

Sorry, friends, you cannot pass "go" until you hear me out on this one. But I promise to make it worth your while.

If you are a human adult under the age of fifty, you have probably considered pursuing a side hustle. Or, at the very least, you've heard the term or know someone who's busy side-hustling as we speak. Now, if you'll recall the pearls of wisdom I shared back in chapter three, they included this big shiny one: "Get a second job." However, a side hustle isn't really a second job, is it?

A hustle sounds like you are dabbling, window-shopping maybe, but not in the game. It is an important distinction.

If you are in the game, then call it a second career and give a goal to that career.

And you know what's self-defeating about all of these side hustles? The "hustle" part. You never actually stop hustling.

I believe that all of the work you do should have multiple purposes. Work sucks, so if you're gonna do it, get the most out of it. Don't just work for a paycheck; work at a place that gives you a paycheck *and* helps you learn a valuable skill. Don't just pick a side hustle that pads your bank account. Pick a side hustle that enables you to reach your larger financial or personal goals.

Pour your limited free time into a side hustle that comes with the opportunity to contribute to a 401(k). (Plenty of franchises offer this to their part-timers.) Pursue something that will help pay for continuing education or get management training. Make sure your side hustle positions you to accumulate assets—either stocks through company-sponsored investment or knowledge and skills—so you're not just trading hours for dollars. Be purposeful and strategic if you're going to launch a secondary endeavor of some sort. Otherwise, you're just spinning your wheels.

Let me give you an example. Say you work a desk job at a big corporation and drive for a rideshare company like Lyft as your side hustle. Aside from learning how to do your taxes as a self-employed person, you're probably not gaining new skills from this gig. You already know how to drive, and you're putting miles on your own car (already a depreciating asset, which depreciates more the longer you drive it).

Lyft has a 401(k) program. Are you using it? How about their financial aid assistance? No? Okay, then, are you taking some of your earnings from driving random people around and sinking dollars into stocks or real estate? If you're not using the assets the company offers, are you funneling that side hustle income into assets of your own?

Now, before you start throwing rotten tomatoes at my head, let me say that I get it. Many desk jobs don't pay people nearly enough, and you might need that rideshare money to pay down your crushing student loan debt. Maybe you send a portion to your family. Side hustles aren't always worked by people who love money; many are worked by people who need money. But even then, there are incremental ways to milk them for assets. Put five dollars per week into that company 401(k). Take just one class. Get the most out of it, however you can.

Here's a story about a rideshare driver who's doing it right.

A couple of years ago, I'm in San Francisco and call an Uber. I hop in and start chatting with my driver, and he asks what I do for a living. (Like ya do.) I mutter something about real estate and he perks right up.

"Really? I'm in real estate, too. That's why I'm driving!"

"Oh yeah?" I say. "Tell me more, man."

So he does. He explains that he and his family live in Sacramento, which is ninety minutes away, but he figured out that if he drove for Uber just one weekend per month in San Francisco, he could make enough for his mortgage payment. (The cost of living is far cheaper in central Cali than it is in the Bay Area.)

I say, "Well, what do you do the other weekends?"

"I bought a rental house," he tells me. "So the money I make driving in San Francisco on two other weekends each month goes toward that mortgage."

See where I'm going with this? See how strategic this man is being with his time and his money and his side-hustling capabilities? He's got a renter paying into the mortgage, and he's making two extra payments on that house himself.

"How about the fourth weekend?"

"Well," he says "sometimes I've gotta rest. But if I work that fourth weekend, I put my earnings toward a trip fund for me and my wife."

This phenomenal fellow also teaches school during the week, and his wife works full-time, so they've also been making double payments on their own house. He's been driving for about a year and has no intention of doing it forever, but for that entire year he'd been making three payments a month on his rental house.

"I should have the rental paid off in four years or less," he said.

I was floored. He had a plan and a vision. He was going to sprint for a few years so he could take it easy for the rest of his life. He was taking the money he made and putting it someplace where it could live and breathe on its own.

This guy was not building a business of his own or investing in someone else's business, so this may seem like a total tangent. It's not, I swear. My message to you is this: If you take up a side hustle, do it with your larger life goals in mind. Don't confuse activity with accomplishment. And while you're at it, acknowledge that launching a successful business of your own may help you move toward those life goals just as quickly, while also creating something that is truly yours.

All right. End of rant. On we go.

Offer a Service or Sell a Product

If you've been bitten by the entrepreneurial bug, you've basically got two choices:

1. **Sell your skills:** If you have extreme or in-demand expertise, you can turn that into a service that pays hourly or in flat fees.
2. **Sell stuff:** If you have a skill that is used to make physical things, you can sell the things instead of your expertise. This encompasses everything from selling food and art to selling exotic plants you've grown or puppies you've bred.

You'll gravitate naturally toward one or the other based on what you're good at, of course. Some of you will be natural-born makers, inventors, and tinkerers who are constantly creating stuff, and some of you will know that your talents and skills are the only things you could ever sell.

But in case you're one of those fantastical creatures who could sell either stuff *or* skills, here's a rundown of some of the pros and cons of each.

SELLING A SERVICE

Pros	Cons
Fewer outright costs to begin with	No assets
No inventory	Fewer expenses to write off
Can sometimes be done without a designated space or office	If you do need a space and business dries up, you're still on the hook for rent
Can be done solo	Can get lonely

SELLING A PRODUCT

Pros	Cons
High growth potential	High cost to launch
The internet makes marketing and shipping items easy	Fees, taxes, and shipping costs add up quickly
The ability to build a brand, a location, or a product into something with loyal fans	As tastes shift, it can be hard to pivot and maintain customer interest
Can be a group endeavor with trusted friends or business partners	Can go horribly wrong if you choose the wrong partners

Neither is easier or better or more likely to succeed. It all comes down to what you want to sell, whether or not it's any good, and how many people want to buy it. Oh, and a boatload of luck.

What's that? You don't think luck has anything to do with the success of a business? How about being in the right place at the right time? Or knowing when the world is truly ready for your idea? I'd bet my hat you've all heard of Chewy.com, the online pet supply company. In 2019, that website went public to the tune of $8.7 billion and raked in an additional $4.85 billion in revenue. Now, if you're an oldster like me, you might also remember a little company called Pets.com that died a spectacular public death in late 2000. Virtually the same idea, but badly executed and launched before the market really understood how to handle supply chain issues in internet sales.[12]

The rise and fall of these companies goes to show that you can have a killer idea or a mouthwatering recipe or a totally unique skill set, but if the timing is wrong or you can't find your market, you will still bomb. So before you dive into building a business, do some market research and customer profiling. Make sure people want what you've got, that they'll pay what you're asking, and that they're ready for it right now. Otherwise, you're wasting your time.

Want to know the easiest way to figure out if people will want what you're selling? Find out if anyone else has made money doing it already. That's right, friends, originality is overrated in the business world, no matter what *Shark Tank* would have you believe. A unique idea or product will certainly grab consumers' attention and might even net you some angel investors, but it'll also make the road to success a long, uphill climb.

If you're making an object or food item that no one's ever sold before, how will you find suppliers? Will you need to build custom parts or order ingredients from all over the world? Even if people say they'll buy your widget, how can you know that they'll commit with their dollars if your widget is the first of its kind? And if you're offering a service, it might be even harder to build momentum. Imagine the first person to open a nail salon or offer their services as a professional nanny. Demanding pay for tasks that people are perfectly capable of doing themselves can be a tough sell. Demanding pay for tasks that people don't yet realize they want or need can be an even tougher sell.

Now, before I dive too far down this rabbit hole, let me pause. I am not saying that if you have a brilliant, 100 percent original idea that's going to set the world on fire, you should abandon it and become a freelance tree trimmer. Nor am I saying that pursuing a business model someone else has already tried guarantees success, even if you do everything in virtually the same way. And the third and final thing I am not saying is that you should steal someone's idea and call it your own.

So what am I saying? I'll tell you: I'm saying that you can be original as an entrepreneur, but you don't have to be. It's far more important to be very, very good at whatever you're doing and to know and leverage your niche.

Be that dog walker who specializes in large or aggressive breeds. Be that bakery owner who only uses recipes from the eighteenth century. Be that freelance editor who works with highly technical subject matter experts and makes their ideas crystal clear. If you don't have a unique idea or a market-creating business model, don't sweat it. Try putting a new spin on an old offering.

Do Your Homework

The only person who can reasonably launch a business without doing some serious research beforehand is a six-year-old who wants to sell crappy lemonade in front of their parents' house. Everyone else needs to hit the books. And the internet. And probably do a handful of informational interviews.

For starters, this business you're thinking of launching is an investment, right? And with any investment, you need to know how much money you will put into it and how much money you can expect to get out of it. Guessing doesn't count, so here's a rough game plan for tracking down some helpful data.

Determine initial costs: Start with the biggest, most important expenses and work your way toward the minutiae. Space will likely be the most expensive item on this list, so research price ranges. How much does it cost to rent in the neighborhood of your dreams? How about buying? Do you need an entire building for your restaurant or a single office for your consultancy? Do you need a custom-built food truck or a powerful array of servers or a table saw? Do you need to secure a patent or a trademark for anything, and, if so, do you need help from a lawyer to make that happen? How much does it cost to set up a limited liability company (LLC) in your home state (in other words, a quick-and-dirty legal classification that will keep your personal assets separate from your business assets, in case you get sued)? This first level of research should focus on space, equipment, and other permanent elements of your business setup. They'll be one-time costs for the most part, except for anything you decide to rent.

Determine any ongoing expenses: Will you need insurance? A license? How often will you need to purchase supplies or ingredients to make your products? How often will you need to advertise to secure customers for your service? If you'll be driving around a lot, how much will you spend on gas each month? If you'll be shipping stuff, can you estimate those costs using the postal service website? I guarantee you won't be able to predict every ongoing expense, but do your best to figure in everything that comes to mind.

Decide if you will hire people and how much they should be paid: This is a tough one. It's easier if you are using a business model that already exists, like a hair salon or a pet-sitting service, since you can either find out how much local competition charges or use careeronestop.org to research average salaries. Otherwise, consider proxies. For instance, if you're going to sell your homemade cookies from a food truck that drives around neighborhoods playing music to lure potential customers, find out how much ice cream truck drivers make. If you need bakers to staff the truck and cook while it rolls, find out how much line cooks or apprentice bakers make.

Decide how much you'll charge: Again, if you're doing or selling something that already exists, scope out your competition. If you're doing or selling something that doesn't exist in the market yet, then research the closest alternative. Or cobble together an estimate from multiple close alternatives. Say you're going to teach people how to joust like medieval knights used to do, but you hit a wall when you realize that you can't just call up King Arthur. Look up how much stables charge to teach people to ride horses, and how much stick fighters charge to teach people combat skills. Somewhere in there is your ideal price point. (Yes, I know that's a nutball idea, but gimme a break. Remember how I said I wasn't an entrepreneur? Now you know why.)

Calculate how much cash you'll need to get started: I highly recommend figuring this part out by talking to someone other than me. If you can schedule an informational interview with a current business owner without ruffling any feathers, do that this instant. If you can't, the US Small Business Administration (sba.

gov) has a fantastic page titled "Calculate your start-up costs," and the Minority Business Development Agency (mbda.gov) offers solid advice on a page titled "How to Estimate the Cost of Starting a Business from Scratch." Of course, you can consult your money mentor, too, but unless they've launched a similar business themselves, they might not have the specialized knowledge you need.

Find out how much money someone who sells a similar product/service makes: As you've probably figured out by now, this research will be a combination of unearthing average earnings from similar business models and educated guesswork. It shouldn't be super hard to find the stats you need, but you should steel yourself for heartbreak. If you've got your heart set on selling your handmade pocket knives online and at craft fairs, but find out most people who sell similar goods make only $18,000 per year, will that change your mind? If you're dying to open a boutique, but find out that 53 percent of small shops fail within four years,[13] are you going to plow ahead anyway? If you launch a business, make sure doing so will actually earn you money. And a decent amount of it.

Don't forget about taxes: As a business owner or self-employed person, you'll have the dubious honor of owing Uncle Sam around 15 percent of each dollar you make. And that's on top of regular state and federal income taxes, so you end up paying somewhere between 30 and 35 percent of your gross income. Most of the entrepreneurs I know set aside 30 percent of their earnings the instant any money comes in, just to avoid a massive tax bill come April 15.

Understand how long it will take you to turn a profit: This'll be tricky, but worth the effort. Since you're likely going to be investing some capital in equipment or space or supplies at launch time, the first round of dollars you rake in isn't going to be actual profit. Instead, that money will be going toward your break-even point. If you're able to guesstimate how much you'll make, on average, for those first few months, you'll be able to figure out when you'll turn your first profit. Most experts say that it takes two to three years for a new small business to start making money,[14] but that's variable depending on your business model. With a restaurant, it'll definitely take that long or longer. If you're working as a freelance consultant who has virtually no overhead, it might only be a couple of months until you're solvent.

Finally, have a strategy to invest any profits in hard assets: This last tidbit of advice comes directly from me, because you know I'm not going to let you consider such a risky, labor-intensive path to wealth without managing those profits wisely. And to me, wisely will always mean less risky, less labor-intensive avenues like real estate, stocks, and mineral rights. You know, all those kick-ass passive income streams we discussed way back in chapter five. Once you've paid your bills, your people, and your debts, sink any leftover cash into investment vehicles that have a half-decent chance of increasing your net worth.

Am I sounding anti-entrepreneur at this point? I swear, friends, I am not trying to crap all over your dreams! I just want you to tackle this with your eyes wide open. Whenever someone tells me they're going to quit their job at a multinational corporation to open a storefront restaurant, I give them the lecture version of the stuff you just read.

I say, "So, you're ready to rent a space, pay for ingredients, apply for beverage licenses, and hire staff? You're ready to own almost nothing related to this business, accumulate zero assets, and sink your energy into a business that won't actually grow? I mean, it won't, since your chairs, dishes, and computers will wear out and need to be replaced fairly often, and since everything in your rented space will take a beating and have zero resale value. And you know that even if a shit-ton of money starts to go through this restaurant, very little of it will end up in your pocket, right? Nearly all of your revenue will go toward rent, payroll, and bills."

And then they give me puppy dog eyes and I feel like an asshole. But I keep going, because dammit, I want people to understand the financial decisions they're making.

"It sucks to realize this, but enjoying the experience of going to a restaurant doesn't translate to enjoying the experience of owning and running one," I tell this poor slob, who now thoroughly regrets asking for my advice.

"Even an operation like a brewery, which creates a tangible product that can be sold and considered an asset, is a better investment than a restaurant. And I'm telling you this as someone who owns restaurants! I love the restaurants I've invested in, but they don't actually make me much money at all. And they certainly don't make their founders into rich folks."

Now that I've given you the lowdown, and you have an idea of how hard it'll be to build a business yourself, here's how to tell if you should continue down this path: Do you still want to? Despite all those dire warnings and potential pitfalls, are you still fired up about your idea? Then do it. Chase that dream. You are one of those rare and fortunate people who is so passionate and determined that you're willing to face shitty odds to carve out a place for yourself in the business world. Be smart and go slowly, but give it your all. You've got my blessing.

Be an Angel

If all those homework assignments and bullet points made you realize that the last thing you want to do is spend years building a business from scratch, welcome to the club. I don't either. Luckily, there are other ways to make money in business that don't involve the blood, sweat, and tears route known as entrepreneurship: namely, venture capitalism.

Venture capitalism is another financial term that most of us only pretend to understand. Luckily, its definition is pretty simple: a venture capitalist (VC) invests in up-and-coming businesses (or ventures) and makes a profit if those businesses succeed. This is also called angel investing, since VCs often swoop in when a start-up is struggling to get real traction, dump a truckload of cash on the business, and make it possible for the founders to forge ahead.

Now, most VCs and angels work for a venture capitalist fund or a venture capitalist firm. A venture capitalist fund is pooled money from multiple investors who work together to research businesses worthy of investment. A venture capitalist firm is just a company that manages a fund. Sometimes VC funds are run by folks who want to support certain types of start-ups, such as those run by women or people of color, or businesses in a specific niche. More often, though, they just want to make as much money as humanly possible as quickly as possible. They want to invest in ideas and models that will turn a profit ASAP so they can replenish the money they withdrew from their fund. They are professional wealth accumulators.

This is another great example of rich people enabling their rich buddies to do big, rich things. While the businesses they fund might be cash poor, the VCs themselves are typically Scrooge McDuck rich and looking to get richer. To them, funding start-ups isn't any different from buying houses or government bonds; it's just another way to make money.

Worried because you aren't part of a VC fund and don't have a truckload of cash lying around right now? Don't be. While most VCs are high rollers, you definitely don't need billions in the bank to help a new business get going.

What you do need is information about promising businesses that need investors. So let's put a new twist on a past assignment. Remember in chapter seven when I made you start some casual conversations among your social and family circles, asking if anyone knew about people looking to invest? Now, hit up those same folks again—or offshoots of those same circles—for information about businesses looking for investors. Does someone have a sister or an ex-college roomie who's trying to get a start-up going? Is there a promising local endeavor that needs an initial pool of cash? Put out those feelers and see what comes back.

On the off chance that's a bust, you can turn to our old friend the internet. Sites such as localstake.com and angelinvestmentnetwork.us would be more than happy to serve as matchmakers between your money and a budding start-up business.

Before you begin your new life as a VC, though, consider how you'd like to be compensated for your investments. Funds and firms make money primarily through the interest that their obscene pool of money makes from the bank, not from the companies in which they've invested. You're an individual investor, so you'll need a different vehicle for your returns. Do you want a share of ownership in the company? A percentage of profits to be paid out each quarter or year? You can certainly hash out the terms with the founder on your own, but you might want to get some help from your money mentor—or even a lawyer—for this one.

As companies grow, they become more complex, so figuring out how much you're owed can get pretty hairy. Better to iron that out when you're writing your investment check than two years in.

Finally, be aware that venture capitalism is far from a sure thing when it comes to making money—or even making back your initial investment. Sink your money into a business that thrives and you could make a fortune. Sink your money into a business that flops, and you get zilch. This is why professional VCs talk about their investments as "bets" and investing as a "game." Offering funding to a brand-new, unproven business is an amazing way to help entrepreneurs' dreams come true, but it's also a gamble. Most VCs get a thrill out of betting on ventures they think will pan out. Most VCs also have money to burn, and you don't. (I'm assuming. If you do, please call me and I can recommend less wasteful ways to fuel your fireplace.)

If the idea of betting on a business scares the pants off you, you're in luck. There's one last way to invest in a venture or company that's far less risky than contributing to its start-up funding: buying stock. You can't do it with small businesses, of course, but it's a simple and relatively reliable way to back a company and be fiscally rewarded for your support.

Get Paid for Telling People What to Do

Let's say you're incredibly good at doing something everyone needs. You know how to fix badly built computer networks or how to teach teams of people to collaborate effectively. You can start a business as a consultant and offer your deep knowledge to clients on a short-term basis, but you'll still have to hustle for business, fork over that pesky self-employment tax, and pay for your own insurance. If the skills you have are truly in demand, and if you're clearly one of the best in the market at applying those skills, you have some other options, all of which have evolved fairly recently.

The first is fractional skill employment. This means offering your services to multiple employers and dividing your schedule among them. You'll work less than part-time for each company and rig up your week so that you're working less than full-time overall. The idea is that you have steady work that allows you to make the most of your deep and in-demand expertise, but you aren't tied to a single company. (And, yeah, it's similar to consulting, but less volatile since most fractional contracts are several years long.)

As a tech dude, I've taken fractional skill jobs myself a few times and loved them. I also know that this model is used in academia, with non-tenured teachers filling positions for one or more semesters and working for multiple universities at a time. But more and more business sectors are opening up to this model, so even if you're not a programmer or a professor, you could make it work. I've seen fractional job listings for scientists, marketers, estheticians, data analysts, mathematicians, and more. Not every skill set lends itself to this setup—I'm looking at you, lion tamers and lumberjacks—but if yours does, you can end up with that sought-after combo of flexibility and stability.

Now, if you happen to have in-demand skills plus a whole lot of charisma, you could also pursue work as a speaker or a trainer. In the pre-internet era, these gigs were reserved for people who had the clout to cozy up to executives or the cash to join a speakers bureau. Today, however, if you've got enough money to buy a custom URL, you can hang out a shingle and offer your services as a keynote speaker, brown-bag lunch lecturer, or a group trainer.

Some HR departments will require fancy certifications for actual trainings—especially on tough subjects like sexual harassment or bullying—but if your area of expertise is something less likely to involve interpreting regulations or laws, all you need is proof that you're a knowledgeable and entertaining speaker. If you can cook up a PowerPoint presentation and forty minutes of material on fashion tips for corporate drones or how to make bike-commuting workable, you can start pitching yourself to all of the corporate campuses in your area.

It helps to have some proof that you've got the chops to entertain a group of worker bees, so consider hiring someone to videotape your first few gigs. Post those to your YouTube channel and website, along with a few testimonials, and you'll have a much easier time convincing folks to hire you.

It also doesn't hurt to have a social media presence and a decent following, which brings me to the final (and possibly easiest) way to make money by telling people what to do: become internet famous.

Did you know some social media influencers make more than $20 million per year? It might take you a minute to build up that kind of revenue, but with a modest following as an influencer, you could bring in $850 to $1,400 per month talking about something you love.[15] The same goes for Instagram—if you're able to gather a sizable audience and create sponsored posts on behalf of corporate partners—and possibly younger social media like TikTok in the near future.

In all of these cases, the idea is to leverage your ideas, expertise, advice, or personality into an online platform. Once you've got a horde of loyal fans, you can explore advertisements, affiliate marketing, sponsored postings, speaking gigs, endorsements, book deals, and more.

If you've got a face made for radio or a serious case of stage fright, try podcasting instead. Popular podcasts that feature advertisements can make twenty to forty dollars for every one thousand listeners,[16] and many hosts ask listeners to contribute via Patreon, further upping their earnings potential. Want to avoid video and audio? If you're a half-decent writer with a unique perspective or useful advice, you can try your hand at blogging. You can make money through ads and sponsored content if you're able to rake in enough page views.

None of these business models existed when I was a kid. If you were extremely smart and a top-shelf expert in something, you could try for a book deal, maybe a TV show, if your area of expertise was weird or titillating enough. But most experts just languished, unnoticed, and mostly unable to make money off their valuable know-how. Now, with so many internet-driven avenues for sharing expertise, smart people with marketable skills can connect with people all over the world who need their help.

Even people with commonplace expertise can get in on the fun. Hell, just imagine having a drippy faucet in 1983 and wanting to fix it yourself. You'd have to either know someone with plumbing skills or hope you could track down the right book at the library to walk you through the process. And now? YouTube has videos on fixing every style of faucet imaginable, narrated in dozens of languages. And the people creating those videos are making money and helping homeowners.

Don't Let Your Business Kill You

Listen, friends. If you are a born entrepreneur, I want you to embrace that. But I do not want you to buy into the myth that launching and running a business must become your whole life. I logged on to Facebook the other day, and a friend had just posted this: "It felt like the more my business grew, the more work there was."

That's not good, and that's not how it has to be. Smart entrepreneurs know how to delegate. Smart entrepreneurs scale their businesses so that the work is done efficiently by a whole bunch of capable people, and the founder can step back. Smart entrepreneurs use their hard-earned money to buy back their time instead of working eighty-hour weeks for decades at a time.

You can build something that can live when you're resting, instead of building something that sucks the life out of you. So if your dream is to launch a business, promise me you'll remember that.

Let's circle back to the caveat I laid out at the beginning of this chapter: I'm not an entrepreneur, a VC, or a YouTuber. I'm way too lazy to build businesses (although I do enjoy funding them). If you gave me a YouTube channel, every video I posted would be ninety minutes long and contain at least five tangents, which might appeal to a very small audience (mostly other Texans) but probably wouldn't make me one thin dime.

I wanted to include this chapter because launching and investing in businesses has always been one of the most popular and important ways to make money. And I want you to make money. But I'm not an expert, so I've done my best to summarize and will now leave you with a nice long list of other books that can help you dig deeper into some of the topics we've barely skimmed in these pages.

The $100 Startup: Reinvent the Way You Make a Living, Do What You Love, and Create a New Future by Chris Guillebeau. In a series of fifty case studies, Guillebeau talks to entrepreneurs who have built businesses earning $50,000 or more from a modest investment (in many cases, $100 or less). When it comes to advice, he focuses on finding the intersection between your expertise and what other folks are willing to pay for. A great primer for anyone who wants to build a company from scratch.

The Young Entrepreneur's Guide to Starting and Running a Business: Turn Your Ideas into Money by Steve Mariotti. Through stories of young entrepreneurs who have started businesses, this book illustrates how to turn hobbies, skills, and interests into profit-making ventures. Mariotti describes the characteristics of the successful entrepreneur and covers the nuts and bolts of getting a business up and running. (And this man should know. He founded the Network for Teaching Entrepreneurship.)

Angel: How to Invest in Technology Startups—Timeless Advice from an Angel Investor Who Turned $100,000 into $100,000,000 by Jason Calacanis. In this book, a Silicon Valley VC guides you step-by-step through the process of becoming an angel investor, covering how leading investors evaluate new ventures and calculate the risks and rewards and explaining how the best start-ups leverage relationships with their angel investors. You don't have $100,000 to throw around? You can still apply some of these principles to smaller investments.

How to Be a Capitalist Without Any Capital: The Four Rules You Must Break to Get Rich by Nathan Latka. I'm going to forgive Latka for using the R-word in his title because this book covers everything from bootstrapping a start-up with almost no funding to investing in small local businesses for huge payoffs. Good stuff.

One Million Followers: How I Built a Massive Social Following in 30 Days by Brendan Kane. This guy calls himself a "growth hacker," and based on his results, it seems like the right title for what he does. He uses this book to teach readers how to build a dedicated online following from scratch, how to create unique and valuable content, and how to create a multimedia brand through Facebook, Instagram, YouTube, Snapchat, and LinkedIn.

CHAPTER
9

What Every Investor Should Know

I'M GOING TO TELL YOU a little secret: none of us was born with the skills we need to be successful investors.

In fact, there's no such thing as a natural-born investor. Even those who are natural-born money savers, or gifted mathematicians, or fearless risk takers have to pay their dues. We all have to research and experiment and fail and spend some time licking our wounds—and then get back up and try again. We all have to spend a long time learning about how to invest before we become any good at doing it. In fact, most folks who eventually become millionaires or billionaires spend their entire lives exploring and learning about the art and science of investing.

That's right, friends, I've already made a bunch of money, and I'm still learning right alongside you. And I'm not ashamed to admit it. Over the years, I've observed that people tend to fall into two basic categories: those who set a goal and then shy away from any learning experiences associated with that goal, and those who are committed to lifelong learning. I'm in that second category.

We lifelong learners wake up every day with the expectation that we must embrace learning in order to expand our toolboxes. I am absolutely and wholeheartedly committed to financial independence, which means I'll actively research and interview and study even when I'm sure I know the answer already. I mean, after you've been investing for more than twenty years, patterns start to emerge and you can make some pretty accurate guesses, but I'm not a huge fan of guessing. I prefer to know. To ask questions and consult experts and be as sure as I can possibly be. That's why I am constantly on the prowl for new information, new shortcuts, new tools, and new strategies. And all of the best investors I know are the same way. They geek out on studying data, and they love to gain new skills or sharpen their old ones.

Ever hear that old business adage "You're either growing or you're dying"? It's one of my favorites, grisly as it may sound, because it points to the vital importance of improving yourself. Not just when you're young, not just when you're in school, but all the time. Every day. Forever.

So, before we dive into this next chapter, think seriously about the aspects of finance, investment, saving, and planning that you know you need to study. Reconnect with your intentions around financial independence and commit to hunting down the knowledge you need to make those intentions into reality. Get brutally honest with yourself about whatever you've been avoiding or whatever skills you've failed to cultivate. Because I don't just want you to learn how to invest, I want you to become a wildly successful, lifelong investor who sets and achieves audacious financial goals. I want you to be one of those shrewd bastards who actually has money instead of just jawing about it in some seedy bar. I want you to put in the time learning so you can reap the real payoff: long-term financial independence.

Got it? Okay, then.

I Learned from the Best

I've told you a lot of stories about my personal history of financial triumphs and tragedies, but what I haven't shared is how I first learned about money. And how lucky I was to learn about it in the way that I did.

My own financial education started a hell of a lot earlier than most people's. See, I was raised by a mom and a set of grandparents who were incredibly smart about managing their money and made sure that I grew up understanding the relationships between working, saving, spending, and investing. I am not kidding when I say I started learning about finances before I'd even started nursery school. Even if I didn't realize it at the time.

As I've already told you, my parents divorced early, and after that it was just my mom and me. My mom educated me about money by being extremely open about it. She would say things like, "I have to go to school today. You're going to stay at day care, but I have to go to school so I can get a good job so we can live by ourselves." She made me aware of the links between concepts like earning a salary and achieving independence.

As for my grandparents, they allowed us to live with them after the divorce, but they never coddled us. And if my mom educated me about money by being open, my grandparents educated me by setting examples through their behavior. For instance, they wouldn't give my mom cash, but they'd buy groceries for her. They told her, "We will pay for more education—a master's degree or whatever you need—but we want you to earn all of your own money."

It may seem like tough love, but I think it was the right thing for them to do. It wasn't that they mistrusted my mom; it was more that they wanted her to feel in her bones that she'd become independent on her own. They wanted her to have her pride, even during tough times when she needed their support.

All this meant that, early on, I saw the link between money and freedom, between earning your own wages and making your own way in the world. That had a huge impact on me, even as a little kid.

Back in chapter three, I shared the story about saving up for Disneyland. How my mom took a second job as a grocery store cashier and put aside twenty dollars per week until we had enough to make the trip out to California. That experience taught me I could set and achieve financial goals. That saving took patience, but it paid off. I learned that working a second job can help you earn faster. That people with no money who made small salaries could still do big things.

Most of all, watching my mom work that shitty second job as a grocery checker taught me about consequences. That spending and saving happen at a cost. That I should always consider the trade-offs. (No airplanes and no hotels, but yes Disneyland? Definitely a trade-off I could make.) That if you want something badly enough, you need to be willing to put in the work to make it happen.

I could spend another fifty pages regaling you with stories from my childhood, but I won't. At least not right now. I'll just tell you this: I learned important lessons about money very early. I thought about money, investing, saving, and spending differently than most kids. I had an advantage, going into the world of investment, because my mom and grandparents were smart and honest about how the financial world works.

Most people aren't that lucky. Most parents don't have the first idea how to give their kids a fiscal education, and that's a shame, but it's also perfectly fine. You're never too old to learn, never too old to change. Especially when it comes to earning, saving, and investing, any time is a great time to explore new avenues.

And that includes right now.

Bust Out the Ranch Dressing, It's Time for More Vegetables

Now that I've tugged on your heartstrings a bit, I need to drag you back to reality. And reality may feel a little harsh, so if you're not in the mood to dig into some serious learning, put the book down and come rejoin us when you have time. We've gotta eat some more vegetables to get through the rest of this chapter.

Why? Because this stuff cannot be faked and it cannot be farmed out. Okay, fine, you can hire some money management whiz to invest on your behalf, but do you really want to do that without understanding what she's up to? Do you really want to entrust her with your earnings and have no clue what she's doing with them? No, you do not, friends. You cannot become a successful investor with your eyes half closed. You cannot become financially independent without understanding the basics of investing. You've got to do your due diligence.

This is the rubber-meets-road stuff, basic mindset shifts and advice that every new investor needs in their back pocket. None of it is super complex, but some of it will frustrate and challenge you, especially if you're impatient, vain, or too caught up in the big picture to worry about details. But believe me, every single nugget of wisdom I'm about to impart will make you a better investor.

Ready to eat some vegetables?

Track Every Transaction

Did you know that there is a 12-step program for people who have massive amounts of debt? It's true. Debtors Anonymous helps anyone who has put their entire life on a Mastercard and has no idea how to get out from under all that debt. And one of the first things they train new people to do is write down absolutely everything they buy. If you pay for it, the expenditure goes in your money journal.

If you're rolling your eyes, stop it right now. Tracking your expenses and expenditures is the one and only way to understand your spending habits. Millionaires do it, businesses do it, and you should, too. Because until you understand how you're spending, you can't make a smart plan for saving and investing.

If an actual money diary doesn't appeal to you, that's fine. Cook up a personal balance sheet instead. This is simply a spreadsheet that includes a comprehensive list of your personal assets and liabilities, tracks the money you've earned and the money you've spent, and gives you a snapshot of your net worth. I update mine monthly and have found that most financially independent people do as well. If you don't want to start from scratch, both Investopedia and The Simple Dollar have tutorials to get you started.

Then, if you're ready to take things to the next level, learn to create a profit and loss statement (P&L). This little beauty is generally used in small business contexts and is basically a financial statement that summarizes the revenues, costs, and expenses incurred during a specified period, usually a fiscal quarter or year. Even if you're not going to launch a taqueria or a marketing firm, this is a skill you will need as an investor. Especially if you go into real estate, like I did. You need to be able to track money coming in and going out so you can plan your next move wisely.

P&Ls can be very simple or extremely complex, so I'd recommend taking an online class or seeing if a local college or university will let you audit a 101-level accounting course. You just need a basic understanding of how businesses account for their spending and, by extension, how to accurately and meticulously account for your own.

Not interested in meticulously keeping track of the money coming in and going out? Too damned bad. Unless you find some mechanism for doing this on a regular basis, you'll never know your true costs of living. And that will get you in some deep shit, and fast.

We've all heard stories about famous athletes and actors, people who bring in all of this money but end up short or broke. Those folks got really good at playing offense; they knew exactly how to bring in the money. But your balance sheet or P&L is where you play defense. It forces you to ask yourself, "Should I be spending money on this? Do I have enough to spend?" and more importantly, "Is *this* the way I want to spend the money that I make?"

Tracking your money is like holding a mirror up to your spending habits. And when you don't do it, you run the risk of forgetting who you are as an investor.

Get Outside Input on Every Deal

I've already warned you that the instant people find out you're an investor, they'll start pitching you. This is exciting. It makes you feel powerful and important. Some of the people pitching you are smart enough to know that, and they'll try to create a sense of false urgency around their pitches. They'll say they only need five investors and that they already have four. They'll say the property has gotten a slew of promising offers already. They'll say their idea or product needs to be bought by a certain date or it'll implode. Who knows? They'll make up any bullshit reason to light a fire under your ass so you hand over your money right now without thinking too hard about it. They'll do their best to sell you the fur-bearing trout farm.

You haven't heard that one yet? Ah, sit back and relax, friends, it's story time.

Picture this: Somebody calls you up and says, "I've got the world's best business idea and all I need is a million dollars from you. Here's what we're gonna do: we'll open up a trout farm."

"A trout farm?" you say.

"Yeah! We can charge admission for people to come in and fish the trout, so that's our first stream of income. Then we're going to put a restaurant right next to the ponds so people can bring the trout they've just caught and we'll cook it for them, right then and there. Another moneymaking idea on top of the admission fees, right?"

"Huh. That's pretty smart," you say, warming to the idea.

"But the two best parts of this deal will blow your mind. First, there's a cat food company that wants to buy the remains of all the trout that we don't use. So we're making money there, too. And! These are fur-bearing trout. So once we skin them, we can make leather goods from their hides!"

Sounded pretty good right up to the end there, didn't it? So good that you might've been willing to overlook that giant red flag and hand over a cool million?

There are two lessons to take away from this story, one minor and one major. The minor one is that the person pitching you has probably thought about every single negative scenario you're going to throw back at them. Good deals are good from top to bottom, and heeding red flags is incredibly important no matter how many rationalizations you hear in response to your questions.

But most of us are emotional critters, and our excitement can get the best of us. Which is why the major lesson here is that it's crucial to get a second opinion on every deal and investment you make. Ask your money mentor to look over the contract. Call your financial adviser before you buy into a new company. Get someone with absolutely no stake in the game to offer an objective viewpoint. Give them $100, take them to lunch, do something to make it worth their while.

Agreeing to terms right after being pitched is extremely dangerous. And it's downright stupid, too.

Which is why you always, *always* need to get a second set of eyes on investments and deals before you sign off or pay down.

Walk Away and Think About It

On a related note, anyone who wants you to do something right now is trying to snow you. Anyone who won't let you get a second opinion or sleep on it is a low-key con artist. Some investment opportunities are time sensitive, of course, but if some dude (or chick or otherwise) insists on pitching to you and taking your money on the same day? That person is not your friend.

Anytime somebody tells me, "You've got to do this right now," I have a standard answer ready to go. I say, "I'm not your guy." And I also clue them in to Piece of Investment Wisdom #2: "I don't put any money into anything without having somebody else who is not connected look at the deal." If they accept those as reasonable terms—because they are—then I consider doing my due diligence and finding out if the deal is worth pursuing. If they get all flustered and start threatening to take this "one-time-only best deal in the universe" opportunity to another buyer, I know I've just saved myself a world of trouble.

Don't Be Afraid to Back Out If You Make a Mistake

A while back, I got a call from a guy who wanted to sell me his house. He's in the area I like to buy in, South Austin and San Marcos, and he's in a house I've wanted to buy for fifteen years because it's next to some properties I already own. In fact, the reason he's got my number is that I always give it to the neighbors around my properties and let them know if they're ever thinking about selling, sell to me first and I'll save them some commissions.

So this fella calls me and says, "Hey, I kept your number for the past few years, and now I do want to sell the house. You still want to buy it?"

And my answer was yes.

Now, that was a mistake, because I hadn't seen the property in person, but I remembered that I wanted the property and that it was next to ones I already owned. And I was out of town at the time so I couldn't just drive over and size it up. So I told him yes. I called my banker. My banker said of course you can buy it and asked me to send him a contract when it was ready. Which I did. I went ahead and signed and sent the owner $3,000 in earnest money.

Then I got my head straight and put Piece of Investment Wisdom #2 into action. I called my real estate mentor and said, "I want you to look at this deal for me. But I think the answer is yes. I'll kick you out a thousand bucks and give you the agent's fee if you go on over and take a gander."

She went to look at it and, being a seasoned pro, saw that there were foundation issues on that house that no normal person would have noticed until the inspection. She also saw a bunch of junk cars in the backyard and what looked like motor oil seeping into the ground.

So was it an unsalvageable disaster? No, but my mentor made me stop and think about this investment.

"How much do you think you'll have to put into this house to get it back to normal?" she asked me. "To rent it out safely?"

And I said, "Well, I figure just about everything costs $10,000."

She said, "Let me run it down and find out the cost for getting those cars cleaned up. And that foundation is definitely going to cost you, so let's get somebody out there to take a look at that before you hand over any money."

Well, here's the kicker. The estimates came back totaling $30,000. The house itself was worth about $200,000. So I would be paying $230,000 for a $200,000 property, since that work would have to be done in order to make the place livable.

So I called the buyer back and said, "If you can take $30,000 off the price, then I'll buy it right now for $170,000. Otherwise, I'm sorry, but I've got to walk away. I said yes before I understood what I was getting into."

And of course the owner gives me a story about how he's got three other people who want to buy that house, with all its safety hazards, right away. Which gives me the opportunity to apply Piece of Investment Wisdom #3 and tell him to go right ahead and sell it to those other jokers. I was *not* his guy.

If you buy up a bunch of bad stocks, you will have to pay some fees to sell them again. If you purchase a certificate of deposit and realize you should've kept that cash liquid, you have to just suck it up. But any investment that involves a contract will have wiggle room. Even if you've agreed verbally or started the initial paperwork, you are very likely to have a chance to think twice and change your mind.

Never be afraid to say, "I've made a mistake; I can't do this." You're always better off walking away from a bad deal than taking it and trying to make the best of it.

Most Good Investments Aren't Glamorous

It is incredibly important to make investments that interest you. If you get into this, do it by choosing the investment avenue that rings your bell or you'll get bored and walk away. Or worse, invest unwisely and lose a bundle.

However, try not to confuse interest and enthusiasm with a need to appear accomplished or in the know. In other words, if you buy stock, don't buy stock in Coca-Cola or Apple. If you're going to invest in a start-up, don't invest in some app that claims to be the next TikTok. Not if you actually want to make money as a newbie investor.

If you just love Apple and are interested in investing in the tech space, by all means, do some research. You'll probably find out that Apple doesn't manufacture the components for the iPhone, and that the same company who makes the cameras for iPhones also makes them for other mobile device companies. Buying stock in that company doesn't have the same cachet as buying stock in Apple itself, but you'll get a lot more shares for your money. And that means you'll earn more, and faster.

Everybody in my area who buys real estate tries their damnedest to snap up houses near the University of Texas at Austin campus. But those properties are expensive and scarce. Me? I buy near second- and third-tier universities. I get more houses and I make more in rent.

Warren Buffett owns GEICO. There is nothing sexy about insurance, and yet he's made a whopping $41.6 billion in profit on this investment. In fact, it's his most profitable investment of all time.[17]

Everybody knows about Facebook and Disney and General Electric. Everybody knows a blue chip stock is safe, and everybody loves to buy up shares of tech's latest darling. If you want to make lots of money over the long term, don't think about glamour. Don't think about name recognition.

Think about adjacencies. Think about who sells office furniture to Facebook campuses. Think about who does maintenance for Disney's theme parks. Think about who is innovating and disrupting markets where GE has fallen short. Teach yourself to look for investments with a consistent run-up rate; companies that have shown steady growth for more than two years, background players who are doing boring shit but doing it really well for a lot of flashy people. That's where the money is. That's where smart investors play.

Glamorous companies and ideas and stocks are where everybody else is investing, and very few of them become millionaires. If you absolutely must own a few stocks in Porsche because it'll make you wildly happy, then do it. But promise me you'll find out who makes their spark plugs and invest in that company, too.

Start Small and Keep Going

Remember the story I shared way back in chapter one about my grand-daddy investing a little money in oil wells so he'd have mailbox money forever? Remember the story from chapter five about the military den-tist who helped me learn the value of putting twenty-five dollars into a mutual fund each month? Remember the story I told you about my mom saving up to take us to Disneyland?

I understand that we're living in an on-demand world right now. We get impatient if a video takes more than three seconds to load onto our phones. We want access to every possible option immediately, we want it cheap, and we want it customized. But investment just doesn't work that way. You cannot make massive amounts of money overnight. Not legally, anyway.

And if I may shove a few more vegetables down your throat, you shouldn't want to do that! Investing is a long game that requires con-stant learning. Making massive amounts of money overnight takes luck, not skill and intelligence. Luck is great when you can get it, but skill and intelligence will serve you far better for far longer. If you want to achieve financial independence, you need to understand what you're doing so you can do it over and over and over again. You need to study and fail and learn from your mistakes. You need to cultivate skills, build a smart team around you, and learn to be patient as you watch your investments grow.

So start small. Be mad about it if you've got to, but start small and start now. Buy a tiny share in an oil well. Put twenty-five dollars a month into a mutual fund. Start saving for a big, expensive trip. And for Pete's sake, keep going. Watch your investment grow and be proud that it's growing. Don't stop and don't give up. That's what most people do, and if you keep going, that will set you apart from the rest of the world and from folks who are living paycheck to paycheck, up to their eyeballs in debt.

Start small and keep going. Be patient as an investor. Nothing will serve you better, I swear.

CHAPTER

10

How to Get Started Investing

MOST PEOPLE THINK LIFE IS "be, do, have." They say to themselves, "If I was lucky and had access to so-and-so's money/talent, I would do something so much better than what they're doing now."

In reality, life doesn't work that way.

You'll *be* something, what you *do* shows up because of that, and what you *have* follows. You need to take action in order to have anything at all, including success, fame, a loving partner, happiness, a healthy body, peace of mind—all the stuff worth having.

You need to let who you are as a person inform your choices and actions. Those actions will lead you to build the life you want for yourself.

If that life includes independent wealth, get ready to work. Yes, I know I've sung the praises of investments that require the bare minimum of oversight, and, yes, I know I have declared myself lazy about five dozen times so far. But you might also have noticed that I worked like a demon as a young man, currently hold a full-time job in addition to being an active real estate investor, and am in a near-constant state of learning. So, "lazy" is relative. And even investments that need little oversight over the long term still require some legwork at the start.

If you believe that real estate is the investment avenue for you, then that legwork will involve lots of independent research, consultations with your money mentor, and reading this chapter until you've got it memorized. Because Uncle Brady is about to give you the inside scoop.

How to Be an Investor

The moment you get paid to do something, you are a professional. Did you make fifty dollars playing a bar gig with your band? You're a professional musician. Did you get paid to revamp your cousin's website copy? You're a professional writer. You might not want to get business cards printed up after just one paid experience, but you can start shifting your mindset and self-image right away.

The same goes for investing. Yeah, there are people for whom investing is their sole moneymaking activity, and they might be Investors with a capital *I*. But investing starts the minute you start getting started. If you've put twenty-five dollars into a mutual fund, you are an investor. If you've sunk $2,000 into a friend's budding start-up, you are an investor.

There's nothing wrong with setting the bar low so you can win now, especially since it will encourage you to continue actively investing.

Remember, just getting in the game is the only step that matters. And once you think of yourself as an investor—the "be" part of the equation—that'll start to drive what you "do" and impact what you eventually "have."

As a side note, Investors with a capital *I* are very real, but they might not conform to the stereotypes you've got lurking in the back of your brain. Investing right now doesn't mirror that classic movie *Wall Street* with Michael Douglas; it's more like the TV series *Billions* with Paul Giamatti. It's less sharkskin suits and more algorithms, less from the hip and more data driven. Today's successful investors aren't interested in just making one or two big bets and collecting an obscenely huge pile of cash. They're dedicated to learning and improving incrementally so they can add to their existing pile of cash a little at a time. Forever.

The great news is that simple software—even a few free or open-source versions—has made it easier than ever to analyze investments and make solid decisions. I still want you to do research, to find a money mentor, and to always get outside input before signing a contract, but there are apps and programs that will make that research and due diligence quick and straightforward.

Being an investor means rubbing elbows with other investors, since you share interests and expertise. But as you begin to recast yourself as an investor, please *do not* compare yourself to others. I'm begging you. There is absolutely no point in finding out whose portfolio is performing best or who owns the most properties. Not only is it a terrible way to conceptualize your own achievements, it'll make you miserable. It'll make you think you are losing. Investing is not a competition, no matter what other investors may say or do.

And they may say some nasty things.

The Three Biggest Mistakes Newbie Real Estate Investors Make

"Oh, so you're a slumlord."

This is what some people—fellow investors and just regular folks, too—would say to me when I told them I invested in real estate. And lemme tell ya, it hurt. For a long time, it stung to hear people reduce my entire life to one dismissive insult. Especially when I started with nothing, learned shit the hard way, and did everything with integrity.

It took me a while to realize that most of the people who called me a slumlord had no idea how real estate investing works. They figured that since I bought low-priced properties and rented them out to low-income folks and students, I was some sort of sketchy con artist. They figured that if I didn't buy houses that I, myself, would love to live in, I was taking my renters for a ride.

I knew they were wrong, but it still stung. Until this one night in La Jolla.

I'd been invited to a gathering of potential investors in La Jolla, California, one of the most expensive residential areas of the United States. And I'm fortunate enough to own a fairly fancy-pants home in Del Mar, which is the sister city to La Jolla, and when I first bought that property, a neighbor said, "Hey, you're new to the area. We have some real estate people getting together at a guy's house in La Jolla on Wednesday nights. He's always looking for investors."

This was fascinating to me. It was the first time ever in my real estate career that someone said, "Hey, I'm getting a bunch of people over to my house because I want to tell them about my investment opportunity and see if they want in." I thought it was genius. So you can bet I showed up to this mind-blowingly huge, Italian-themed mansion with a swimming pool and a big-ass waterfall in back. I showed up with all my wealthy neighbors and listened to this guy named Frank give his spiel. He was roughly my age, plainspoken, a nice guy.

He got up and said, "Hey, everybody, thanks so much for joining me here at my house. My wife and I are delighted to have such a great crowd. Now you all know that I'm really here because I'm looking for investors, so let me get right to it."

He gave us a little presentation on his business and holdings, which was a little dry but not too shabby. And a few minutes in, he said something that knocked me flat. He told us that he owned more than four thousand rental houses across the United States. And he pulled up some slides of his properties, and damn if they didn't look just like the ones I buy for myself! They were modest, low-priced rental houses in undervalued but solid markets like Toledo, Ohio, and Tulsa, Oklahoma. He was looking for investor money so he could buy another three thousand of them and keep them in this bond on Wall Street.

And I was flabbergasted. I thought everybody who was a big-time real estate person was the anti-Brady. I figured they were buying massive buildings and ornate castles and fancy golf courses. And this guy? Who lived in an ornate castle? His average rental property was in the $150,000 range.

He told us, "The reason why I'm in this business is that the people who are in these types of homes tend to rent for long periods of time. They're low to middle income, starting their careers or finishing school, and they tend to stay put for at least five years."

"That's my exact renter profile," I thought.

I was knocked out. I mean, it was one of the best, most validating days of my life. I'd just been told that a moneymaking model I'd been using for decades was also being used by other savvy investors with integrity. And once the presentation was over, and I got to chatting with the other guests, I quickly found out that many of them had the same profile: they owned a bunch of homes that they wouldn't want to live in right now, but certainly would've lived in at a different time in their life when they were just getting started. And many of them were multimillionaires.

I finally made my way over to Frank and couldn't resist spilling my guts.

"Frank, I've gotta tell you something," I said. "I don't know if I'm going to put any money in with you, but I will definitely send people your way because I believe in what you're doing."

I told him about my houses. I actually pulled up one of them on my phone and he said, "Oh yeah, I'll buy those all day. Do you want to sell them?" Rich guy jokes, right?

I asked, "Hey, do you ever get called a slumlord?"

And without blinking, the guy goes, "Yeah, they used to call me a slumlord. But now they call me a hedge fund billionaire."

And it changed me. It changed me even though I knew I wasn't a slumlord. It changed me to get that concrete reminder that being good at real estate investing didn't have to mean buying up high-rises in Manhattan or mansions in the South of France. Smart investors know that smart investments aren't always glamorous.

In fact, the first real estate lesson is this: you do not have to buy properties that you want to live in yourself. That's a huge mistake. Just like me, you can buy properties that aren't up to the standards of your current self, but would have been perfect for your student self, or your just-getting-started-in-adulthood self, or your fallen-on-hard-times-for-a-bit self.

Doing this doesn't make you a slumlord. It makes you a smart investor who is helping responsible renters find decent housing.

The second mistake that new investors make is buying houses that are one gust of wind away from falling down and spending mountains of money on repairing them. Not smart. Those repair costs need to be recouped. You'll get out from under your debt and mortgage much faster if you buy houses that need minimal or no repairs and start renting them ASAP. Before you buy anything, be sure to run a return-on-investment (ROI) analysis and fold in any renovations or repairs.

Basically, an ROI is a set of calculations that help you determine if what you invest will be recovered by what you expect to earn back. How's this for a weird example? You buy a pedigreed cat for $5,000 and plan to breed her. If she has two litters of kittens each year, and each litter has at least three salable kittens that you can sell for $5,000 apiece, you can expect to make $30,000. Even if you have to pay a $2,000 stud fee to breed her with some fancy tomcat twice, you're still bringing in $26,000 on the deal. So you'll earn back your initial investment of $5,000 and make a healthy profit. (Rental properties seldom have kittens, so your ROI calculations will involve things like property taxes and rent income, but hopefully you get the picture.)

Finally, a favorite that's come up in previous chapters but bears repeating: for the love of all that's holy, do *not* manage your properties yourself. Unless you plan to own or start your own property management company, there is no reason for you to be the person your renters call when the furnace poops out. Hire a property management company or a trusted individual to do it for you. Be a real estate investor, not a landlord.

Three Types of Profit You Can Make from Real Estate Investments

I'm what is known as a buy-and-hold investor. Once I invest in a property, I keep it. More or less forever. So the main type of profit you think of when you think of real estate—the profit made off the sale price—doesn't really apply to me. And if you go the buy-and-hold route, it won't apply to you, either.

But! You will have access to three other types of profit so long as you invest wisely and keep a meticulous P&L sheet going.

1. **Appreciation:** Real estate will always be worth more over time. Yes, even though the housing market implodes occasionally, the trajectory of real estate investments is still heading steadily upward. This means that every house you buy will gradually be worth more. And even though you may never sell those houses, their increased value gets applied to your overall net worth, which impacts your ability to borrow. It's not money in your pocket, but it's still incredibly valuable to you as an investor.

2. **Equity:** There are two parts to every mortgage payment. One is the interest, which is the bank's fee for loaning you money. And the second part is equity, which is the piece that you paid yourself, or what's commonly called the down payment on a note. Most people don't recognize this, but that equity that you pay in—or more importantly, that your renters pay in—is a form of profit for you. Even if you didn't make a profit this month that you can put in your savings account, you made a profit in principle because someone else paid down your asset. And after twenty years, they will have paid off your mortgage for you. Whenever your renters pay into your equity, that is pure profit.

3. **Positive cash flow:** As I've mentioned, it will take a long time before you see any meaningful cash flow from your rental properties. Smart real estate investors use the rent money they receive to cover mortgage payments and other costs, and don't pocket any of it. But once the mortgage is completely paid off, you'll be able to collect some cash each month when the rent rolls in.

You're going to fixate on number three. I know you are. And that's natural. But promise me that you'll do your damnedest to incorporate one and two into your understanding of real estate investment. Because when you realize you're making a profit on three fronts, and that your profits are steadily increasing over time, it becomes a hell of a lot more fun and rewarding.

Financing Is Your Friend

If you fixate on cash flow, as I suspect you will, you may also decide that you won't buy any properties until you can pay for them outright. That way, you'll start making that sweet, sweet rental income sooner, right?

Technically. But here's why I want you to borrow to buy instead.

Let's pretend that you have $100,000 in cash just collecting dust and decide to pay for a whole building outright. Here's a ridiculously oversimplified version of how your annual cash flow might work.

Property price	$100,000
Income from rent	$14,000
− Expenses	-$4,000
Net	$10,000

Not bad, not bad. You made a 10 percent return on your investment in one year, which is better than you'll get on most other investments. But now let's see what you can do with a smaller down payment.

Let's pretend you start with $3,500 and get another $6,500 from two buddies. Now you can put down 10 percent, or $10,000, and borrow the remaining 90 percent of the $100,000 purchase price. If the mortgage on the property is 5 percent, your monthly payment will be $483, which changes your annual cash flow quite a bit.

Income from rent	$14,000
Expenses	-$4,000
Loan payment	-$5,796
Net cash flow	$4,204

Whoa. That's *way* less than the $10,000 you made when you paid cash for the building. But in terms of percentages, you're actually ahead. Paying all cash, your net return was 10 percent. In this scenario, you only forked over $10,000 in cash (versus $100,000), and $4,204 is 42 percent of $10,000. Your return on investment just skyrocketed from 10 percent to 42 percent.

Not only that, but if you can afford to roll most of that rent money back toward paying off the mortgage, then you're accruing equity with someone else's dime. Your renters are paying back the bank for you. Why not run things that way so you can make your cash go further, sink it into multiple down payments for multiple properties, and start building your real estate empire like a proper tycoon?

No Flippers

Listen to me right now: TV has poisoned your mind. They've made flipping houses look enjoyable, easy, and profitable. It is none of those things. Taking a fixer-upper and transforming it into a stylish home takes blood, sweat, tears, time, and money. Which is why I avoid it and recommend against it.

I say this and I share the guilty pleasure of watching those shows occasionally. TV also has constraints of production that make showing actual timelines very difficult.

If you turn on the *Johnny and Janie Flipper Show*, they'll tell you that this mastermind couple bought a house for $100,000, painted and tidied it up in a single weekend, and sold it for $120,000—which means they got a net gain of $20,000. Right? Real simple math.

But that's not what happened. Not here in the real world.

What really happened is Johnny and Janie bought the house for $100,000. Then they had to buy paint, new hardware, light bulbs, maybe some new carpeting, or an appliance. Those things don't come free. Let's make up a number and say that all the repair supplies they needed cost them $5,000. Now they've spent a total of $105,000 on this house.

So they sell it for $120,000. To make that possible, they had to pay the real estate agents and the title company approximately 10 percent of the sale price, plus a boatload of bank fees. Let's say that eats a flat $12,000 out of their sale price. Which means Johnny and Janie only get $108,000 on the sale. And since they spent $5,000 fixing it up, it's actually $103,000.

So it sounds like Johnny and Janie only made $3,000 on the deal. But in reality, they didn't even make that much. Know why? Because it took two months to flip the house. And if we say the mortgage payment was $1,000 per month, that means they had to come up with an additional $2,000 out of pocket. (That's called the carrying cost.)

So how much did Johnny and Janie make on the $120,000 flip? A cool $1,000. And that's if you don't count the time and energy that they poured into it, possibly including days off work for the repairs and various closing meetings.

And that, my friends, is why I don't flip. That is why I buy and do virtually nothing to my properties, unless it has to be done. While the flippers make tiny cash profits on massive amounts of work, I make ongoing appreciation, equity, and cash profits on relatively little work. If you want my sage advice, flip only if you have a competitive advantage to the market.

Where to Look for Investment-Worthy Real Estate in Your Area

As a novice real estate investor, you may be tempted to buy up properties wherever you can get 'em. You'll start scouting markets with universities or blue-collar populations concentrated in specific neighborhoods, and think, "Hey, I could make a killing out in Albany, New York!"

If you've thought along those lines and don't live in Albany, New York, yourself, please read this next section very carefully.

When you start buying properties, a good idea is to buy in smallish towns with high populations of renters, but those smallish towns should be in your geographic area. Even though you won't be managing your properties yourself, you should *buy* properties in an area that you know. It should be somewhere that's got a culture and interpersonal dynamics that you can understand, and in your home state, so you have a chance at understanding the laws and regulations.

Not only should you buy close to your own home, I recommend buying in clusters. I really only have properties in two or three areas near Austin, and over time I've become intimately familiar with those areas. I know how long people stay in their houses, how they treat those houses, and how they treat their neighbors. Which makes me an informed buyer when new deals come on the market.

When you're picking your own two or three areas, it's not a bad idea to focus on neighborhoods that have schools. Elementary schools are fantastic, as they tend to attract stable families who rent for long periods of time, but colleges and universities are great for their student populations.

After you've been buying properties for several years, and understand how being a rental-property owner really works, you'll be able to spot a house that fits your criteria from an online listing. You might even get to the point where you don't need to do a walk-through personally, since all houses in your target profile are pretty much the same. Since you've concentrated your buying efforts in two or three areas, you now know those areas inside and out. Over time you'll find yourself spending as much time learning area stats as analyzing individual deals.

Speaking of analysis, there are some truly fabulous tools for understanding neighborhoods from afar. Start with the US Census website's sections on income and census growth to find out which areas are prospering and attracting new people. Check local Chamber of Commerce websites to find out if new businesses are moving in, and how often they're shutting down. Snoop around university websites to find stats on their student body growth; schools that are expanding will need more housing, after all. And bear in mind that you'll need to do this research on your own. Local real estate brokers typically will not be able to give you stats at this level.

There are just too many mistakes to be made when you buy in areas that you don't personally know or understand. Buy in your own town. Buy what you do know. Monitor nearby areas using current tech. There is likely enough viable real estate within five miles of your first rental property to make you into a career investor.

Remember Your Balance Sheet!

And now, another lesson in commonly misunderstood mathematics. Just because a property looks good and might make money if it was sold outright doesn't mean it'll make a cash profit month to month. At a bare minimum, your rental income must cover management fees, maintenance, mortgage costs, and property taxes on each building you buy. And some properties have great prices and high market value, but won't rent out for the right amount of money to cover your costs.

Remember the bankruptcy attorney who did me a solid back in chapter one? When he helped me sort out the giant mess I was in back then, one of the things he said to me was, "I'm going to give you the properties that will make you money. And I'm going to give the court the stuff that won't make you money but is worth more."

I was speechless for a moment.

I said, "Are you telling me that some of the most valuable stuff I own won't make any money when I rent it?"

"Yeah, and since you didn't know that, you clearly need to learn a thing or two about cash flow," he said. "Your low-end properties—the ones that have lower value in the market—are the ones that have all the monthly cash flow. You have some expensive properties that are worth a pretty penny on the market, but you're actually losing money on them every damned month."

In other words, he was telling me to cook up a P&L and study it regularly.

And, now, that's what I'm telling you. To be a successful real estate investor, you must understand where you can make a profit. You must understand which houses will rent for the appropriate amount to cover your costs. You will learn these things by studying, crunching the numbers, and making mistakes, but the more studying and number crunching you do, the fewer mistakes you'll need to make. Before you ever buy your first property, sketch out a plan for how you'll manage its financial needs over the next one, two, five, and ten years. Create a P&L and update it every month, if not more often. Monitor when you earn and when you spend and when you need to borrow.

Never make a financial decision without having a full and clear picture of your current financial standing.

Finally, an adage that I didn't create myself but that I repeat annoyingly often: The best time to buy real estate was twenty years ago. The second best time is now. Doing something now is almost always better than doing nothing. If real estate excites you, start reading, start tracking down a mentor, start saving for that first down payment. Inertia is real. Get started. Get going. Take action so you can find out who you can *be*, what you want to *do*, and what you'll end up *having* as a lifelong investor.

CHAPTER
11

Why You Should Get Started as an Investor

GETTING STARTED AS AN INVESTOR is intimidating. I get that. The idea of taking money that you earned and putting it into something other than a bank account is just weird and scary if you've never done it before. But here you are, reading this book. And that tells me you're curious. And if you're curious, that means you're probably open to experimentation and trying new things. So try this. Try investing. Put twenty-five dollars into a mutual fund. Pool your savings with some friends for a down payment on a rental property. Research and buy a few stocks. Try it out. Do it now.

Why? So many reasons. But here's a couple.

Because Investing Works for Everyone

I'm a big fan of Sammy Hagar, and not just because Van Halen is a kick-ass band. Sammy is a super talented musician, but he's also self-aware and a smart, shrewd businessman. In his memoir, *Red: My Uncensored Life in Rock*, he explains that he knew early that the music business was just that—a business. However, he could see that the booms and busts could provide occasional large sums of cash to use for other projects.

So he started investing. He built businesses. He bought bicycle shops and turned them into multimillion-dollar endeavors. He told *Inc.*, "When we started touring a bunch, I started my own travel agency so I did not have to pay someone else fees to book our travel." Cabo Wabo, his tequila brand, was acquired by Gruppo Campari in 2010 for $91 million.[18] He also owns Cabo Wabo Cantina restaurants in Mexico and the United States, as well as a chain of airport restaurants and a fine-dining establishment.

Now, this is a guy who—like me—grew up poor and never wanted to be poor again. So he was investing his earnings from the moment his music career started taking off. He knew that not everyone can be a genius or a superstar, but anyone with time, patience, and discipline can be independently wealthy.

Because Life Is Short

At some point in my Zig Ziglar phase, I came across this idea and it stuck. Zig pointed out that we each have only 27,000 days in our lifetimes. And every millionaire is acutely aware that they only have so many hours in each day. That may sound morose or pessimistic, but what Zig was trying to get at is the value of time. The importance of spending our time in ways that reward us. The perspective we need to take to understand that we spend nearly all of our time working to pay for our expenses, and very little of it actually enjoying ourselves.

So if you've only got 27,000 days to work with, think about the end and work backward. Do you want something more than working a nine-to-five job until retirement, so you can finally have fun when you retire at age seventy-two? Do you want something more than working long hours for paychecks that barely cover your expenses? Do you want something more than one vacation every five years? Do you want something more than a tiny apartment you don't even own?

If you do, you need to invest. You need to think about ways to buy your freedom earlier, faster, and more efficiently than you could ever do on a corporate payroll.

Because Your Day Job Likely Won't Take Care of You

Back in chapter three, I told you about my friend who spent an entire year prepping for a promised promotion because his boss, a VP, had a "plan." Then the company "changed directions" and his boss's promise vanished into thin air.

Even great companies run by fantastic people with huge hearts can't be trusted to steward your financial future. They are responsible for the company's profit margins and responsible for their own finances. They'll do their best for you, but it'll never be enough. It'll never help you build the life you've dreamed of living.

Another mentor with knowledge of the corporate world said something I've always felt, even when I've been working my tail off at corporate day jobs. He said, "You can never cut a deal with a man at a corporation. He may not be in the same job the next time you see him, and the next guy coming in behind him doesn't know who you are." I realized he had a point. What I needed were mentors who could help me build my own thing. He advised that I needed debt in order to grow and create, which can be terrifying. Finding people who had the life I wanted and who would help me find my own path to that life helped me take control over my trajectory.

Corporations and steady jobs are fantastic for the multitudinous reasons we discussed in chapter three. But you have less control over what happens at a company than you do over your own individual investments and endeavors.

If you want to be free, you've got to build something for yourself.

Because an Extraordinary Life Takes Work

Remember my mom moonlighting at the grocery store so we could go to Disneyland? She took some sideways looks and even derision from the local community for that. The small minds in our small town liked to look down their noses at her for working a blue-collar job, even though she had a college degree. But she knew that working a second job was the only way to make possible the life she envisioned for herself and for me. Her teaching job just didn't pay her enough, so she found a way to earn more so that we could live bigger lives. Better lives.

If you want an extraordinary life, you can work toward it. In fact, you've got to work toward it. It won't fall in your lap or materialize out of thin air. But if you think carefully, act strategically, invest wisely, and never stop learning, you can create it.

As an investor, you will have the ability to shape your present and build your future. And who wouldn't want that?

EPILOGUE

One More Note Before I Hit the Surf

IN THE WORLD OF MONEY, people understand that there is always a trade-off between time and, you know, money. That means the best possible source of income is passive income, since it requires very little time to make a profit and can profit for years to come. The second best is salary or commission income. The third is hourly-wage income, where you're trading your time for a relatively low rate of pay. And, of course, the worst option is unpaid labor, which should be avoided unless you can see some future benefit that is not readily apparent in the numbers. This is me, reinforcing a lesson from that final chapter: that how we spend our time matters.

Now, this is me reinforcing it with a story.

Back in college, I took a class on government. The subject was interesting and the professor was sharp, and one day she did something totally fascinating.

It was a Monday, and without much ado, she came walking into the lecture hall, set down her bag, and looked out at the class.

"Hey, how many of you guys saw the football game yesterday?" she asked.

I'd missed it myself, but I bet 60 percent of my classmates' hands went up.

And she said, "Wow, that's interesting. More than half of you tuned in. What was the final score?"

She did a little Q&A, asking for details about the game, which my fellow students were happy to answer. This got everybody chattering happily, eager to talk about anything other than federal institutions.

"How long did the football game last?" she asked.

Somebody said, "About forty-five minutes."

She said, "That can't be right. There's all the commercials and commentary. I mean if you just sit down in front of the TV and watch from start to finish, how long would it be?"

"It's about four hours," someone shouted.

"Got it," she said and wrote four hours on the board.

"Did some of you watch more than one game this weekend?"

"Oh yeah, Saturday and Sunday."

"So eight full hours watching football over two days," she said, writing those numbers on the board. "Well, how many of you don't miss a single football game all season?"

Let's say that 50 percent of the students in a 300-person auditorium confessed to watching every football game they could see on television.

The professor then proceeded to do the totals. With two games per week totaling eight hours, four weeks in a month, and about five months in a football season, she estimated that 50 percent of my classmates were spending 160 hours watching football games on TV.

"That's a whole week you're spending in front of the tube, and that's just the amount of time y'all are spending watching football during one part of the year," she pointed out. "All those hours spent worshiping at the altar of somebody else's career. Do you realize that not one of those foot-ball commentators, team owners, or players is ever going to come visit you in the hospital or pay your bills if you don't have a job? This is a one-way street here. You're pouring your precious time into watching those games and getting virtually nothing in return. Watching football isn't making you smarter, or helping you build relationships, or getting you any closer to your goals."

Everyone started muttering.

"Listen, I'm not saying that you shouldn't relax or do things that you enjoy. I'd never say that," she said, putting down her marker. "What I'm saying is you might want to go home and think about how you choose to spend your time. Are you spending it on somebody else, or are you spend-ing it on yourself and your goals?"

And then she adjourned class and sent us away.

I have no idea why she felt compelled to teach us that lesson on that day—much less what the hell it had to do with the government—but it changed me. I stopped watching television. I made a conscious effort to trade the hours I used to spend watching television for something more productive. I would read one more book on investing. I would do an informational interview with one more investor. I would use my limited free time to actively move toward my goal. That professor made me check my honesty, check my mindfulness, and be more conscious of my actions. In that one short lecture, she taught me that every choice I make matters.

Now that I've done informational interviews with dozens of wildly successful people, I can safely say that every single one of them is mind-ful about how they spend their time. Successful people work hard. They dedicate themselves to their goals. You don't get to be Stephen King by binge-watching *Game of Thrones*. You don't get to be Warren Buffett by spending every weeknight in front of a baseball game. You don't become a financially independent investor by vegging out.

You have to do the work. You have to hone the skills. You have to dedicate yourself to a lifetime of learning. You have to be mindful.

In fact, do everything mindfully. Because a lot of people out there are in the business of keeping you distracted. All they want is for you to spend hours and days of your life mindlessly zoned out in front of that screen. And they're never going to do a damned thing for you. They're going to suck up as much of your limited and precious free time as you'll give them.

So the next time you sink into the couch to let three-hour-long episodes of some show wash over you, think twice. The next time you let the hours slip by as you scroll endlessly through social media, force yourself to stop. This is your one and only life. And your goals aren't gonna crush themselves.

What can you do differently? What trades can you make? What are you going to change that will make those goals not just possible, but inevitable?

Whatever it is, you should be doing that instead.

For me, being mindful about spending my time in ways that serve my goals has enabled me to write these final words from beautiful Hanalei Bay, Kauai. What is the outcome you will not be distracted from? Pursue that and be mindful of the things that are competing for your time. Cheers to finding it.

Brady Johns
Kauai, Hawaii, 2022

ACKNOWLEDGMENTS

THANK-YOUS TO Kevin Anderson, Sally McGraw, and Matt Holt for guidance and encouragement.

Thank you, David Cole, for fifty years of friendship and the expert legal advice along the way.

Special thank-yous to Luther Gabe Biondo and Justin Jackson for twenty years of staying on me to get this written. The world needs more friends like you.

Author's Note: I had three mentors named Tom, and there is some license taken in the examples in this book. For instance, I may have heard the same advice from two and chose to meld stories for impact. The intent is to acknowledge their guidance and impact, and express my gratitude.

Any errors or omissions are mine and not theirs.

Tom Sapp, Tom Davis, and Tom Haley—Thank you.

ENDNOTES

1. Amanda Dixon, "Survey: 21% of Working Americans Aren't Saving Anything at All," Bankrate, March 14, 2019, www.bankrate.com /banking/savings/financial-security-march-2019/.

2. Walter von Saal, "Selected Data on Aging," employees.oneonta.edu /vomsaaw/w/psy345/handouts/demograf.pdf.

3. Jennifer Calfas, "Americans Have So Much Debt They're Taking It to the Grave," *Money*, March 22, 2017, money.com/americans-die-in -debt/.

4. "Planning & Progress Study 2019," Northwestern Mutual, https:// news.northwesternmutual.com/planning-and-progress-2019.

5. Celebs Life Reel, "Blair Eadie," celebslifereel.com/blair-eadie/.

6. Madeline Berg, "The Highest-Paid YouTube Stars of 2019: The Kids Are Killing It," *Forbes*, www.forbes.com/sites/maddieberg/2019/12 /18/the-highest-paid-youtube-stars-of-2019-the-kids-are-killing -it/#6b66fb3038cd.

7. Celebrity Talent International, "Danielle LaPorte Profile," www .celebritytalent.net/sampletalent/18266/danielle-laporte/.

8. Gary Henderson, "How Much Does Influencer Marketing Cost," DigitalMarketing.org, www.digitalmarketing.org/blog/how-much -does-influencer-marketing-cost.

9. Maurie Backman, "A Shocking Number of Higher Earners Still Live Paycheck to Paycheck," The Motley Fool, www.fool.com/retirement /2020/03/04/a-shocking-number-of-higher-earners-still-live-pay .aspx.

10. Berkshire Hathaway Inc., "2013 Shareholder Letter," https://www .berkshirehathaway.com/letters/2013ltr.pdf, accessed Jan. 26, 2022.

11. Peter Applebome, "The Hunts: A Dynasty Built on Poker and Oil," *New York Times*, August 30, 1986, www.nytimes.com/1986/08/30 /business/the-hunts-a-dynasty-built-on-poker-and-oil.html.

12. Andrew Beattie, "Why Did Pets.com Crash So Drastically?" Investo-pedia, October 31, 2021, www.investopedia.com/ask/answers/08 /dotcom-pets-dot-com.asp.

13. Gerald Hanks, "Types of Small Businesses Likely to Fail," *Chron*, smallbusiness.chron.com/types-small-businesses-likely-fail-63862 .html.

14. Ellis Davidson, "The Average Time to Reach Profitability in a Start Up Company," *Chron*, April 9, 2019, smallbusiness.chron.com /average-time-reach-profitability-start-up-company-2318.html.

15. Werner Geyser, "How Much Do YouTubers Make?" InfluencerMar-ketingHub.com, October 19, 2021, influencermarketinghub.com /how-much-do-youtubers-make.

16. Joe Pinsker, "Why So Many Podcasts Are Brought to You by Square-space," *The Atlantic*, May 12, 2015, www.theatlantic.com/business /archive/2015/05/why-so-many-podcasts-are-brought-to-you-by -squarespace/392840/.

17. Billy Duberstein, "Here's How Much Money Warren Buffett Has Made in GEICO," The Motley Fool, December 29, 2019, www.fool .com/investing/2019/12/29/heres-how-much-money-warren-buffett -has-made-in-ge.aspx.

18. Liz Welch, "How I Did It: Sammy Hagar," *Inc.*, November 2013, www.inc.com/magazine/201311/liz-welch/sammy-hagar.html.

ABOUT THE AUTHOR

 Brady Johns is a real estate investor who owns more than thirty residential and commercial properties and a global tech executive whose résumé includes tenure with three of the world's most storied companies: Google, Sun Microsystems, and Dell. He's traveled to more than sixty countries, climbed the highest mountain on four continents, hiked volcanoes, swum with whale sharks, and run several marathons. He has many more destinations on his wish list, but most days you'll find him researching real estate, stocks, and cryptocurrencies while grabbing breakfast tacos in his hometown of Austin, Texas. A born teacher with a huge heart, he hopes that his first book's mix of funny, heartwarming stories and practical financial advice will reach a new generation of investors who struggle to manage their earnings. Feel free to follow Brady's adventures on Instagram @bradyjohns.